Shifting Gears

Shifting Gears:
Changing Labor Relations in the U.S. Automobile Industry

Harry C. Katz

The MIT Press
Cambridge, Massachusetts
London, England

This book was set in Palatino
by Achorn Graphic Services Inc.
and printed and bound by Halliday
Lithograph in the United States
of America

Library of Congress Cataloging in Publication Data

Katz, Harry Charles, 1951–
  Shifting gears.

  Bibliography: p.
  Includes index.
  1. Collective bargaining—Automobile industry—
United States—History.   2. Wages—Automobile
industry workers—United States—History.   3. Qual-
ity of work life—United States—History.   I. Title.
HD6976.A82U528   1985   331'.04292'0973   84-26105
ISBN 0-262-11098-9

To Jan

Contents

List of Figures

List of Tables

Acknowledgments

I am grateful to many people for their help. Peter Cappelli, Tom Kochan, Debbie Kolb, Bob McKersie, and Paul Osterman read an early draft of this book and each provided a long list of helpful suggestions. My knowledge of the auto industry and thoughts regarding its development also have benefited greatly from discussions with Irving Bluestone, Mike Piore, Chuck Sabel, Harley Shaiken, and Jim Womack. I also learned much from the managers, union officials, and workers who graciously welcomed me into their plants and told me their stories.

Financial support was provided by the Sloan Foundation. I also received financial assistance from the Lilly Endowment and the German Marshall Fund through my participation in the M.I.T. International Automobile Program. Alan Altshuler and Dan Roos, codirectors of the M.I.T. program, supplied encouragement and advice. And when I reflect on the origins of this book I realize that this book in many ways derives from an interest in labor issues and a perspective inspired by the training I received from Lloyd Ulman.

I dedicate this book to my wife. Without her moral, financial, and intellectual support this writing would not have been as much fun and may not have been possible.

Shifting Gears

1   The Need for a Labor Relations System Framework

Under the pressure of an enormous decline in sales and employment, a number of unprecedented events occurred in labor-management relations in the U.S. automobile industry between 1979 and mid-1983. These events included the negotiation of pay freezes as part of a number of efforts to stave off the bankruptcy of the Chrysler Corporation in 1980. Early renegotiation at General Motors (GM) and Ford of national agreements with the United Autoworkers (UAW) in 1982 also produced unprecedented wage and fringe benefit concessions. Meanwhile news stories began to report that the spread of plant closings and the fear of further employment declines had led to negotiation of major work rule concessions at the plant level. There were also reports that efforts to reverse the decline of the industry had led to the replacement of the traditional adversarial relationship between labor and management with a new cooperative spirit. It was said that in many plants the development of this cooperative spirit was linked to the growth of programs focused around improving the quality of working life (QWL) in the plants. Some observers went so far as to suggest that these developments amounted to the emergence of a new industrial relations system in the United States (*Business Week* 1982).

Yet by early 1984 questions began to be raised as to whether conclusions regarding the emergence of a new industrial relations system had been premature. In the second half of 1983 auto sales increased sharply, and then in the winter of 1984 Chrysler, GM, and Ford announced significant profits for 1983 and forecast sizable profits in

1984. As labor and management at GM and Ford renegotiated national labor contracts in September 1984, the press began to question
whether the traditional adversarial relationship between labor and
management had rebounded, along with the industry's financial
status. Some observers pointed to Chrysler's 1983 national agreement
with the UAW and recent indications of increased shop floor militance as clear signs of the return to traditional collective bargaining.

Labor relations developments in the U.S. auto industry have received
a lot of attention from the press in part because the auto industry is a
major employer and has strong links to a number of other major U.S.
industries. In 1979, broadly defined, national motor-vehicle-related
employment was 8,053,000, or 8.3 percent of the total civilian labor
force.[1] Attention also focused on the industry because the auto industry had earned the reputation as an innovator within U.S. labor relations by developing many of the now-common features of U.S.
collective bargaining agreements. For example, the 1948 GM-UAW
agreement was the first major industrial labor agreement to include a
cost-of-living adjustment (COLA) escalator as part of a multiyear contract. Then in 1955 the auto industry pioneered the use of supplementary unemployment benefits and in 1976 introduced paid personal
holidays. The innovative role and importance of the auto industry to
U.S. industrial relations has extended much beyond specific contractual terms. The course of collective bargaining in the auto industry
throughout the postwar years was widely publicized and helped pro-
pel the industry into the role of a pattern setter with regard to the
general form and style of labor-management relations (Kassalow
1981; Harris 1982).

Attention was also drawn to the auto industry because the changes
underway there appeared to be representative of those being introduced in so many other unionized industries. In recent years many
of the nation's leading industries have adopted pay concessions,
work rule changes, and worker participation programs similar to the
changes underway in the auto industry. These industries were often

facing the same environmental pressures that plagued the auto industry—heightened international competition and greater instability and uncertainty regarding future prospects.

Yet, as in the auto industry, the upturn of the U.S. economy raised fears that traditional bargaining would return in these industries. Academics joined this debate, with Dunlop (1982) and Mitchell (1982), among others, arguing that concessionary bargaining had happened in one form or another in the midst of earlier recessions and would disappear in this case as it had in the past when recovery ensued. But others, including Piore (1982), Freedman (1982a), and Kochan and McKersie (1983), saw significant new developments and signs of fundamental change in labor relations conduct. The question at issue in this debate is whether the pay and work rule concessions and cooperative programs adopted in the auto and many other unionized industries in recent years are a temporary response to economic troubles or set in motion a new pattern of behavior likely to persist in the future.

The purpose of this book is to clarify this debate by analyzing whether a major transformation is underway in the conduct of labor relations in the U.S. auto industry. To understand whether recent changes in auto labor relations add up to a major transformation, it is necessary first to understand the traditional labor relations system that operated in auto collective bargaining. Once the traditional operation of that system is clarified, it is possible to discern whether recent pay concessions and worker participation programs entail a major modification of traditional auto labor relations or whether they merely continue the long history of minor amendments to this system.

The theoretical framework guiding this book is the view that labor-management relations in the auto industry (and other industries) are a product of environmental pressures and the strategic choices made by labor and management in the context of those pressures.[2] As this book will show, in the context of a particular set of environmental constraints, labor and management in the auto industry developed in the post–World War II period a well-defined and interconnected labor relations system characterized by three key features: the determination of wages through formula-like wage rules in multiyear agreements, a connective bargaining structure that defined the relationship between national and plant-level bargaining; and a job control focus operating at both national and local levels premised on the contractual and arms-length resolution of disagreements. By the early 1950s these key features were all in place and until the late 1970s produced outcomes consistent with the desires of both labor and management and the auto industry's economic environment.

This is not to say that from the time when the key features of the auto labor relations system were introduced until the late 1970s the actions and strategies adopted by labor and management were irrelevant to the interests of the auto firms or autoworkers. Rather the three key features served to structure and guide the course of auto bargaining. In the auto bargaining system there was room for actions and periodic amendments to the bargaining system, all of which had serious consequences for the system's operation and outputs; however, the three key features interrelated and reinforced one another in a manner that shaped outcomes for labor and management and limited the extent and impact of amendments to the system.

Throughout my analysis of the traditional collective bargaining system and recent changes in that system, much attention is paid to the functions served by either particular system features or changes in those features. This analysis repeatedly focuses on understanding the needs any given bargaining feature served for either labor or management. It is my view that a clarification of the functions served by the various features of the auto labor relations system is the key to explaining the process of collective bargaining.

Like the seminal work of John Dunlop (1958), my theoretical framework recognizes the central role that economic pressures exert as an environmental factor shaping the design of industrial relations systems. And like Dunlop, in my view a central task of industrial relations research is to explain the differences among industrial relations systems and the factors inducing change in industrial relations practices.[3] The perspective on collective bargaining adopted in this book is also similar to Dunlop's framework in that it views collective bargaining as a mixed-motive relationship. In this view management and labor are seen as driven by the tensions between integrative and distributive bargaining, to use the terminology of Walton and McKersie (1965). This leads to the result that the parties are sometimes able to agree to cooperative efforts to increase the available joint gains, but the success of those efforts inevitably is constrained by each party's attempts to maximize its own gain and the mistrust that arises as a consequence of those efforts.

My theoretical framework differs from Dunlop's in two important respects, however. My perspective stresses the need to explain the dynamic changes underway in an industrial relations system. This book analyzes the historical evolution of the U.S. auto collective bargaining system and the factors that shaped that evolution. In addition I recognize that in designing the auto bargaining system and in their recent introduction of changes to that system, labor and management have some choice in their decisions. Dunlop, and many other industrial relations researchers who followed him, held to the view that industrial relations systems were all converging to a common form, a view most clearly expressed in *Industrialism and Industrial Man* coauthored by Kerr, Dunlop, Myers, and Harbison. With the view that pressures for convergence were dominant, Dunlop and other industrial relations researchers downplayed analysis of the dynamic changes underway in industrial relations systems, the important role played by historical factors in shaping this dynamic evolution, and the significant differences that persisted in industrial relations systems across countries.

In recent years a number of social scientists have moved away from the focus recommended by Dunlop and convergence theories and have shifted their attention to clarifying and explaining the large diversity that exists across the industrial relations systems of the leading industrialized countries. The work of Piore, Dore, Sabel, and Cole stands out as examples of this literature.[4] This research discusses the factors that structure industrial relations systems and the source of differences in these systems. The research points out the critical role of factors such as the extent of economic dualism, the reliance on external labor markets versus lifetime employment principles, and the role of cultural and ideological differences in workers' attitudes. A central focus in this research is the attempt to distinguish between the importance of historical versus cultural factors as a determinant of the form of industrial relations systems.

This book follows the lines of recent social research by identifying the factors that structured and guided the U.S. auto bargaining system. As a result I focus on the broad rules and features that structured auto collective bargaining, such as wage rules, connective bargaining, and job control unionism, in contrast to Dunlop's alternative consideration of collective bargaining rules.[5]

This book is different from comparative social science research in that I focus on explaining the historical dynamics of one particular industrial relations system. I am less concerned with explaining how and why the U.S. auto collective bargaining system differs from practices in other countries and more concerned with understanding the factors shaping the evolution of the auto system within the American context. In addition, in the social scientists' debate regarding the relative importance of economic versus cultural factors, I emphasize the role of economic factors.[6]

My methodology uses historical, case study, and statistical analysis. This is another characteristic that distinguishes this book from earlier industrial relations research. Historical analysis is critical to my efforts to understand the evolution of the bargaining system in the auto industry. Case study analysis is also used to understand recent events in the industry, in particular the cooperative programs and work rule changes adopted at the plant level. The changes in work rules and cooperative programs I observed in visits to a number of plants are described later, as are developments in a few illustrative plants by way of more extensive case descriptions. In addition statistical analysis is used to assess the interrelationship between industrial relations performance and economic performance. This data analysis, utilizing plant-level data from two divisions in General Motors, is also helpful in evaluating the impact of the cooperative programs in place in the 1970s and the role such programs might play in the industry's future response to international competition.

Mixing methodological approaches provides an understanding that might be missed by using only one methodological technique. Historical analysis clearly is necessary to understand the dynamics involved in the auto bargaining system's design and evolution. And yet to assess the impact that the variation in noncontractural shop floor practices exerts on economic and industrial relations practices, the quantitative cross-sectional data analysis is crucial. Case study analysis is essential to track and identify the scope of recent changes underway, and the interviews conducted as part of the case studies clarify the attitudes of workers and labor and management officials regarding new programs. Research that relied exclusively on quantitative analysis of industrial relations and economic performance indicators would be hard pressed to uncover these attitudes or the subtle implementation problems that arise in shop floor changes.

Another important feature of my analysis is that it focuses on labor relations in the so-called Big Three auto companies: General Motors, Ford, and Chrysler. The book does not specifically discuss labor relations in the supplier segments of the industry outside the Big Three and only occasionally refers to labor relations practices in other U.S. auto companies such as the small, independent companies still around in the 1950s, or American Motors, or Volkswagen's U.S. plants in operation in the 1970s.

Some developments underway in the auto industry may be slighted by this focus. I concentrate on the Big Three in part because labor relations in those companies strongly affected bargaining elsewhere in the auto industry by way of pattern bargaining, whereby contract terms in the major companies were extended to the other final assembly companies and to the supplier industry. Also it was the national collective bargaining agreements negotiated at the Big Three that introduced contractual innovations to the U.S. industrial relations system and served as a pattern setter to other industries along other dimensions. Furthermore most of the recent shop floor innovations and worker participation programs were first introduced in the Big Three. Consequently focusing on the auto collective bargaining system as it operated in the Big Three provides an accurate assessment of the major historical developments while also providing a good basis for speculation regarding the future course of auto industrial relations.

Chapter 2 describes the three key features and the historical operation of the auto labor relations system in detail. A critical part of this chapter's description of past auto bargaining entails clarifying how the three key features of the labor relations system interacted with and reinforced one another. It is the existence of this complex interaction across the three features that makes it possible to speak of a labor relations system in auto bargaining.

An important aspect of the operation of the traditional labor relations system in the auto industry, and a defining characteristic of any other system, is that problems are dealt with through amendments to and modification of parts of the system and not through major reorganizations of the system. Chapter 2 illustrates that prior to 1979, each of the three features of the auto bargaining system was periodically modified in this fashion. Amendments made to the traditional system include occasional diversions of formula wage increases and the variation allowed across plants in work rule bargaining.

With an understanding of the earlier amendments made to the auto labor relations system, it becomes possible to compare these earlier adjustments to the changes that emerged between 1979 and 1983. Chapter 3 describes the changes made to the wage rules, local work rules, and the connective bargaining structure after 1979. This analysis reveals that recent wage and work rule modifications go beyond the scope of earlier amendments.

Analysis of the evolution of QWL type programs and case studies of the cooperative programs in a few illustrative plants are presented in chapter 4. The early QWL programs were additional amendments to and not a fundamental alteration in the traditional system. These programs had a limited focus and centered around efforts to manage the tenor of labor-management relations and the aspects of that relationship that were not strictly bound by contractural rules and procedures. Yet after the industry's downturn in 1979 and, in particular, in plants that adopted a team system of work organization, new forms of worker participation began to produce major movements away from the industry's traditional job control orientation. Chapter 4 analyzes the team system and the challenges it poses for labor and management.

Quantitative assessment of the interaction between plant-level industrial relations and economic performance is provided in chapter 5. Plant-level data from two divisions in GM over the 1970s are used to measure this interaction and the impact of early QWL programs on economic and industrial relations performance.

Where is the U.S. auto labor relations system heading? What impact will changes in labor relations have on the industry's growth and economic performance? Chapter 6 turns to these issues. In line with my theoretical framework, which stresses the importance of the eco-

nomic environment, analysis of the likely course of the U.S. auto
bargaining system requires speculation regarding future economic,
technological, and other environmental pressures. As in the past,
however, environmental pressures will shape the alternatives facing
labor and management in the auto industry but will not strictly determine the course of labor relations as labor and management make
strategic choices regarding future labor relations developments. This
leads me to consider the various strategic options available to labor
and management.

The strong interconnections among the various key features of the
auto labor relations system limit the range of choices available to labor
and management. Labor and management must choose among a few
discrete alternative labor relations paths. Chapter 6 traces the outlines
of these alternative paths and relies on recent strategic choices made
by labor and management to help predict future choices.

If they choose to reshape their bargaining relationship, labor and
management will likely look to practices of foreign producers for
alternatives and a new labor relations model. In particular they probably will look to procedures and processes used in the Japanese and
West German auto industries, which have been relatively successful
in competing with U.S. companies. For that reason my analysis of the
alternatives available to the parties in the United States and likely
future U.S. developments considers the lessons to be learned from
the Japanese and West German labor relations systems.

Will the auto industry continue as an innovative force and in the
process provide an example that will help other U.S. industries respond to heightened international competition? Or in the face of unsuccessful efforts to reform its own conduct, will the auto industry
suffer economic decline and provide an example of failure rather than
one of promise? The final chapter of the book addresses these questions by tracing the extent to which other unionized industries are
facing environmental pressures similar to those in auto and the de-

gree to which those other industries appear to be copying innovations developed in the auto industry.

Although the auto industry historically has functioned as a pattern setter in the U.S. industrial relations system, there are certain characteristics that set collective bargaining in auto apart from labor relations in other industries. The auto industry differs from a number of other industries because of the high level of unionization and the fact that one union—the UAW—dominates it. In other industries in the United States, the significant growth of nonunion firms has emerged as a major environmental pressure on union firms in recent years, a pressure largely absent from the auto industry. In addition the bargaining structure in the auto industry is relatively centralized. The extent to which any of these or other factors set the auto industry on a particular course or places constraints on future labor-management developments in other industries is addressed in the final chapter.

Even in the face of these differences, I argue that the labor relations system operating in the auto industry can be viewed as a model of the system that governed labor relations more generally in the United States over the postwar period and as a model of the kind of changes now underway. Readers might find it useful to keep this claim and any differences between auto and other industries' collective bargaining in mind when reading through my characterization of auto collective bargaining.

But, in order to assess whether the recent changes made to auto labor relations will amount to a fundamentally new course and point the way for other U.S. industries, it is first necessary to provide some historical perspective.

Key Features of the Auto Collective Bargaining System, 1948–1979

The work rules, wages, and fringe benefits comprising or regulating the working conditions of the hourly work force in the auto industry are delineated in collective bargaining agreements negotiated by the UAW and the management of each company. These collective bargaining agreements, since the mid-1950s in the form of three-year agreements, are long, detailed documents. For example, the 1982 national agreement between the UAW and Ford is four volumes, each roughly two hundred pages in length. Volume 1 outlines such issues as scheduled wage increases, the seniority system, and the grievance system. Volumes 2 and 3 describe the fringe benefits, including the pension, insurance, and supplementary unemployment benefit systems. Volume 4 outlines a series of supplementary letters of understanding between labor and management that interpret and in some cases extend the other contractural language. For each auto plant there is also a local plant collective bargaining agreement describing additional work rules and terms and conditions of employment, typically of another 150 pages in length.

One could analyze the nature and course of labor relations in the auto industry by tracing the evolution and implementation of the many detailed clauses within the national and local agreements. Alternatively one could choose a particular contractual item such as pension benefits and study how negotiators in one or a series of bargaining rounds negotiated and reached final agreement over the terms of the item. Much would be learned by such an analysis. But by adopting such a narrow focus, one would lose sight of the continuity maintained in bargaining over time and across the industry.

In this and the chapters that follow, I do not analyze all of the detailed adjustments made in the contracts between the automobile workers and the auto companies over the post–World War II period. Rather I focus on the three key features of those agreements that have served to structure the relationship between labor and management. It is my view that only by understanding the evolution of these three key features of the auto industry's labor relations system can one fully understand both the workings of the system and the nature of the recent changes made in response to the industry's dire economic situation.[1]

The three key features are wage rules, connective bargaining, and job control. In terms of subject matter the domains covered by these features are the compensation package, the continuity of bargaining within and across the auto companies, and the extent and way in which workers and their union participate in decisions.

Wage Rules

Formula-like mechanisms have been used to set wages in collective bargaining agreements in the auto industry since the GM-UAW agreement in 1948.[2] The formula wage-setting mechanisms regularly included in the national contracts are an annual improvement factor (AIF) and a cost-of-living adjustment escalator (COLA). The AIF increased wages at 2 to 3 percent per year, while the COLA automatically raised hourly wages in accordance with increases in the nationwide consumer price index.

History and Operation of Wage Rules
In the immediate postwar years labor-management relations in the auto industry, as in much of U.S. industry, were extremely unsettled and marked by a series of long strikes.[3] In part the unsettled nature of

labor-management relations resulted from the end of the war and the lifting of wage and other regulatory controls exercised by the National War Labor Board and other wartime agencies. Within the UAW at this time there also was underway a struggle for the national leadership of the union, pitching a young Walter Reuther against a more left-leaning coalition led by George Addes. The struggle had been taking place throughout the war, but the removal of the influence of the War Labor Board fueled the fight.

In the fall of 1945 Reuther led GM workers into what turned out to be a protracted strike. Reuther demanded a 30 percent increase in wages to make up for declines in living standards induced by wartime inflation and War Labor Board wage controls. Reuther also demanded that GM open its books so as to allow for inclusion of discussion of pricing and profits as part of the negotiations while at the same time alleging that GM could afford a sizable wage increase without any accompanying increase in car prices.[4] During the strike President Truman appointed a fact-finding panel to examine the dispute, and the UAW responded by maintaining that ability to pay was a proper factor in any decision of the panel.

Pressure mounted on Reuther to settle the strike after the steel industry set a pattern for this round of bargaining by following President Truman's recommendation for an 18.5 cent wage increase. Eventually the 1945–1946 strike ended at GM when the UAW accepted the steel industry's pattern wage settlement. Although the steel agreement served as a pattern setter in this bargaining round, from 1945 to 1950 no one industry attained the status of a full-fledged pattern leader in collective bargaining, nor was there the kind of interindustry pattern bargaining that was to emerge in later bargaining rounds.[5]

Political battles underway in the CIO and the UAW added instability to the postwar negotiations. During the 1945–1946 strike Reuther was criticized by others in the CIO for his aggressive bargaining demands. Then in 1947 Reuther's efforts to improve on GM's offer of an 11.5

cent per hour wage increase were undermined by an agreement on those terms between GM and the United Electrical, Radio and Machine Workers who were rivals of Reuther and trying to increase their relatively small membership in the auto industry. Later the continuing unsettled nature of auto bargaining was signaled by a 103-day strike at Chrysler.

It appears that labor and management in the auto industry were struggling to find procedures and agreements that would stabilize their negotiations. Free-for-all negotiations had produced long and unpredictable strikes that were draining the financial coffers of the auto companies, the workers, and the union. A major innovation that served to remove some of this instability came in 1948 from Charles Wilson, president of GM. Apparently while recuperating in the hospital, Wilson fashioned the idea of offering the AIF and COLA formulas to the union as part of a multiyear agreement.[6] Management made the offer, and it was accepted by the union and incorporated into the 1948 GM-UAW agreement.

In the 1948 agreement the AIF was set at 3 cents per hour (per year), roughly 2 percent of the auto assembler's average hourly wage. The COLA escalator provided a 1 cent per hour wage increase for every 1.14 point increase in the consumer price index. For the assembly line worker this COLA formula amounted to full cost-of-living protection (every 1 percent increase in the rate of inflation, as measured by the consumer price index, generated a 1 percent automatic COLA increase in wages in addition to the AIF increase).

Amendments to the Wage Rules
In national contract negotiations from 1950 to 1979 occasional modifications were made to the wage rules, but these modifications were made in a fashion preserving the structure of the rules. For example, the AIF increase was raised to 4 cents per hour per year in the five-year 1950 agreements. Then in 1953, after the UAW pushed

for a living document interpretation of the national contracts, the agreements at the Big Three were voluntarily reopened. In the new agreements the AIF was raised to 5 cents per hour, the COLA formula was revised, and skilled workers received an additional 10 cents per hour. The AIF then varied between 2.5 and 3 percent of average hourly earnings in the three-year national agreements reached between 1955 and 1967. From 1967 until 1979 the AIF formula provided 3 percent annual wage increases.

After 1955 the COLA formula was revised periodically in the national agreements. By the early 1970s the COLA escalator provided roughly 80 percent coverage for inflation (a 0.8 percent wage increase for every 1 percent increase in the consumer price increase).[7]

The COLA and AIF formula-generated wage increases occasionally were partially diverted to cover the costs of the rapidly expanding fringe benefit package. In the 1964–1967 GM-UAW national contract, the first year of the AIF wage increase was eliminated with the rationale that it was needed to assist in covering the costs of the expanded health and life insurance benefits provided in the agreement. In the 1967–1970 Ford-UAW national agreement 1 cent of the scheduled COLA was eliminated so as to cover the costs of an additional holiday added to the fringe package, and in the 1979 agreements at Ford and GM 14 cents of the scheduled COLA increases was diverted to cover the costs of fringe benefits.

Periodic amendments to the wage rules included the negotiation of wage increases on top of the formula increases for skilled trades workers. Pressure to do so came from the skilled workers' threats to secede from the UAW in the late 1950s and from the large wage increases received by construction trades workers in the private sector in the late 1960s and early 1970s.[8] Negotiators responded to these pressures by providing skilled trades workers with an additional 30 cents per hour in 1967 and 20 cents per hour in 1976.

The only time the form of the COLA and AIF formula increases was significantly amended was in the 1967 national agreements, a change that subsequently precipitated the longest strike in the industry since the tumultuous immediate postwar period. In the 1967 national agreements a cap was placed on the COLA formula, limiting the COLA hourly wage increases to a maximum of 8 cents per year. Rapid rates of inflation in the late 1960s then led to the generation of 26 cents per hour in accumulated COLA increases that were not granted because of the cap on the COLA formula. Subsequently in its 1970 contract negotiations with GM, the UAW adamantly demanded that the 26 cents in forgone COLA increases be added to the 1970–1973 contract and claimed there was an understanding in the 1967 negotiations providing for such an eventuality (Serrin, 1973). A sixty-six-day strike followed, settled only after GM agreed to the union's demands to add in the 26 cents and reinstate an uncapped COLA formula (along with continuing the 3 percent AIF).[9]

All of these cases modified either the COLA or AIF but did not alter the structure or central importance of the wage formulas. On the whole the important fact was how rigidly the wage rules were applied. Consequently there was no explicit linking of wage setting to the short-run employment consequences of wage levels.

One could have imagined the development of contract negotiations that produced the negotiation of high wage increases during periods when the auto industry was prospering or appeared to be entering a period of prosperity. In this system wage growth could have slowed or even reversed when financial and employment conditions (or prospects) worsened in the industry. It should be remembered that the U.S. auto industry endured sharp swings in output, employment, and profits over the postwar period. The volatility in level of employment of production workers in the motor vehicle industry (SIC 371) in the postwar period is illustrated by figure 2.1. Yet wage setting was not sensitive to these short run employment fluctuations.

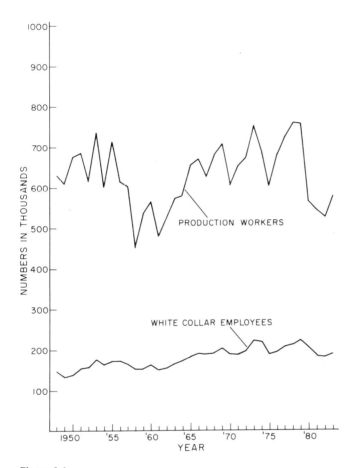

Figure 2.1
U.S. auto employment (SIC 371), 1948–1983. Source: U.S. Department of Labor
(various years).

Consistency of the Wage Rules with the Economic Environment
The stated intent of the AIF was to give autoworkers the benefit of technological progress.[10] The original 3 cents and later 3 percent figures for the annual AIF increases were chosen so as to match the rate of productivity increase underway in the general economy.

To test for the success and strength of the wage formulas, one can compare the actual wage increases paid to an auto assembler to the wage increases that would have matched the sum of full cost-of-living protection plus the increase in the economy's productivity. The $1.44 per hour assembler's wage in 1948 would have increased to $11.11 in 1981 if workers had received full cost-of-living adjustments and real wage increases equal to the actual economy-wide growth in productivity. In fact the assembler's hourly wage was $11.45 in 1981. In the 1970s although the actual COLA formula provided only an 80 percent coverage for inflation, parity was achieved because the COLA short-fall was compensated by the fact that the 3 percent AIF increase exceeded actual economy-wide productivity growth, which had slumped to 1.8 percent per year.

This calculation reveals how closely the wage rule matched the economy's rate of productivity increase and inflation combined. This suggests one of the primary reasons why labor and management accepted the continuing application of the wage rules: their consistency with broad economic trends. In addition the wage rules were consistent with the economic health of the auto industry reflected in the long-run rise in domestic auto production (figure 2.2).

Another economic reason for continuation of the wage rules is that until the 1970s, they produced a steady relationship between the earnings of autoworkers and other blue-collar workers in the U.S. economy. Table 2.1 reports the ratio of the hourly wage rates received by assemblers in the auto industry and the mean hourly earnings of all production workers in the private sector. From 1950 until 1965 the ratio varied between 1.17 and 1.19.

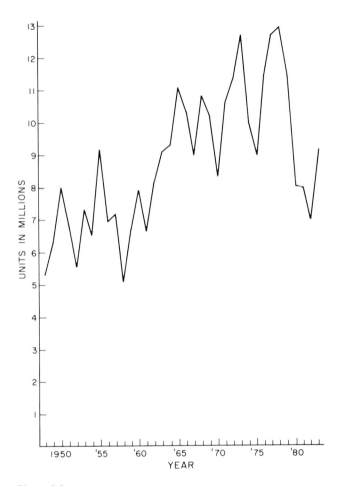

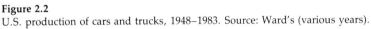

Figure 2.2
U.S. production of cars and trucks, 1948–1983. Source: Ward's (various years).

Table 2.1
Comparison of hourly earnings of auto assemblers and all production workers in the
private sector, 1948–1980

	Auto Assembler[a]	Average Production Worker in the Private Sector[b]	Ratio
1948	$ 1.58	$1.23	1.29
1950	1.58	1.34	1.18
1955	2.01	1.71	1.17
1960	2.46	2.09	1.18
1965	2.91	2.45	1.19
1970	4.25	3.22	1.32
1975	6.44	4.54	1.42
1980	10.33	6.66	1.55

Sources: Assembler data from U.S. Department of Labor (1979a) and Ford Motor
Company (1979). Private sector data from U.S. Department of Labor (1983d).
a. Hourly earnings (including COLA and AIF) of assemblers at Ford Motor Company.
b. Average hourly earnings of nonsupervisory production workers in the nonagricultural private sector.

Then in the late 1960s and 1970s autoworkers' earnings increased
sharply relative to average earnings in the United States. Inflation in
the late 1960s and 1970s had led to a fall in the real earnings of many
workers as the U.S. economy adjusted to the shock of sharply rising
energy and food prices.[11] The continuation of the COLA and AIF
formula increases protected autoworkers from the effects of these
price increases and produced the reported relative increase in
autoworker earnings (to 1.55 of mean earnings) by 1980.

Fringe Benefits
Along with these increases in real hourly earnings, autoworkers received steady improvements in their fringe benefit package. The high
cyclical volatility in auto demand along with the rigidity of wages led
to a large-scale layoffs and recalls over the postwar years. In response
labor and management negotiated a system of recall rights based on
plant-level seniority agreements, which determined the distribution
of these layoffs among the hourly work force. In addition supplementary unemployment benefits were negotiated in the national UAW

agreements in 1955, which were improved in the 1967 and subsequent agreements. These supplementary payments were provided in addition to state unemployment insurance payments and as of 1967 provided 95 percent of take-home pay for up to fifty-two weeks to laid-off autoworkers. The availability and size of the unemployment benefits served to reduce the problems generated by layoffs and thereby supported the continuation of the wage rules by reducing the pressure to respond to cyclical declines in the industry through wage cutting.

Over the postwar period fringe benefits became a larger share of total worker compensation. Table 2.2, reporting the hourly compensation costs to GM of an auto assembler, shows that from 1948 until 1980 real total compensation and fringe benefits rose, respectively, 313 and 1,177 percent.

Like the setting of wage levels, the negotiation of these fringe benefits proceeded in a structured manner. Fringe benefits were not negotiated in a flexible manner in response to the short-run financial or employment conditions in the industry. Rather they were added in sequential steps. The evolution of the fringe package was influenced strongly by demands from the UAW that emerged over long periods of time and in response to long-standing campaigns by the union

Table 2.2
Total hourly compensation costs for an assembler, 1948 and 1981

	1948	1981
Base wage (includes COLA and AIF)	$1.44	$11.45
Fringe benefits (includes social security, insurance, holiday, and vacation costs)	.18[a]	8.20[b]
Total	1.62	19.65
In 1948 dollars[c]	1.62	6.28

a. This figure is taken from MacDonald (1963, p. 40).
b. This figure is an estimate calculated by General Motors Corporation. (It is consistent with other estimates that have circulated recently in the industry press.)
c. The consumer price index rose from 72.1 in 1948 to 279.3 in 1981.

leadership. The pattern was that after a long campaign by the union, a particular fringe benefit would be added to the national contract. Then in subsequent negotiations the union would push for the extension and elaboration of the benefit.

The negotiation of supplementary unemployment benefits (SUB) illustrates this pattern. The demand for some form of guaranteed annual wage appeared on the UAW's platform as early as 1937 (McPherson, 1940, pp. 103–105). There was an income security plan in place in GM as of 1939 that paid laid-off workers benefits out of future earnings, but the union continued to find this plan inadequate. Reuther repeatedly raised the demand for a guaranteed annual wage in the immediate postwar negotiations (Harbison and Dubin 1947). In the early 1950s the UAW commissioned an advisory panel of academics to study the issue and offer recommendations. Then in the 1955 contract negotiations a SUB plan was created (first at at Ford), which went a long way in satisfying the union's demand for greater income security and stability. A SUB fund (funded solely out of corporate contributions) at first provided laid-off autoworkers with 65 percent of their take-home pay for four weeks and then 60 percent for twenty-two weeks. In the 1967 contract renewal the SUB benefit was extended to a maximum benefit of 95 percent of take-home pay. (The 65 and 95 percent figures include any available state unemployment insurance benefits.)

The union's demand for a reduced work week followed the same evolutionary pattern. Demands for a reduced work week first surfaced in the immediate postwar bargaining rounds and were later repeated throughout bargaining in the 1950s and 1960s (Harbison and Dubin 1947, p. 92). Sometimes this demand surfaced in the union's request for a four-day work week. Finally the union was partially successful; the paid personal holiday benefit introduced in 1976 provided autoworkers with twelve unscheduled days off over the term of the agreement in addition to regular holiday, vacation, and sick days.

In the 1979–1982 contracts at Ford and GM, the number of paid personal holidays was expanded to nine per year.

One might expect to find that major fringe benefit innovations (or breakthroughs) occurred only in the midst of production peaks or upturns; however, analysis of the history of fringe benefit improvements finds only limited adherence to this pattern. Figure 2.3 plots the major fringe benefit advances against the industry's total production of motor vehicles. The figure shows that the introduction of some fringe benefit innovations did follow a pro-business cycle pattern. For instance, the introduction of $100 per month pensions (in addition to Social Security) and company payment of one-half of the costs of medical and life insurance were won by the UAW during national contract negotiations that occurred during a short-run peak in domestic production in 1950. The 1955 contract negotiations, which brought the introduction of SUB benefits, also occurred during a cycle production peak. In line with this pattern, the 1958 negotiations, which occurred in the midst of a sharp downturn in auto sales, did not include any fringe benefit innovations and, rather, saw management reject Reuther's request for the introduction of profit sharing.

Yet a number of fringe benefit advances also occurred in the national negotiations that took place during auto sales downturns. A major victory for the UAW was the extension of SUB benefits from 65 percent to 95 percent of take-home pay that occurred in 1967 during a short-run sales downturn. In addition, thirty and out pensions (those allowing retirement after thirty years of work independent of age) were first partially introduced in the 1970 negotiations, which also occurred during an auto sales trough. Another example is that paid personal holidays were introduced in the 1976 negotiations, which shortly followed a sharp drop in auto sales in 1974 and 1975.

The record suggests that the bargaining and tactical skills of labor and management negotiators did influence the exact form and timing of the fringe benefit improvements. The strikes that occurred in national

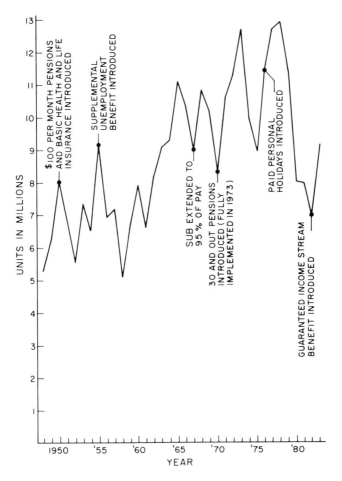

Figure 2.3
Chronology of fringe benefit advances. Source: Ward's (various years), U.S. Department of Labor (1979a, 1979b).

contract negotiations over the postwar period often involved a test of wills regarding the size and form of the fringe benefit package. However, a structure was provided to this tactical bargaining by the fact that fringe benefit settlements had to be consistent with the long term ability of the major producers to pay. In addition structure and continuity were added to these negotiations by the union's long campaigns over major fringe benefit advances.

Functions Served by Wage Rules and Continuity in Fringe Negotiations

One of the functions served by the formula COLA and AIF increases was to provide orderly adjustment of wages during the multiyear national agreements. In that way the use of wage rules was closely linked to the creation of multiyear contracts. The fact that the parties shifted from a two-year agreement in 1948, to a five-year agreement in 1950, and then to a three-year agreement in 1955 attests to the experimental nature of their efforts to arrive at a satisfactory contract and wage-setting form.

A second, and in many ways even more important, function of the use of rules to guide wage and fringe benefit determination was that the rules greatly reduced the potential scope of disagreement over compensation and provided a structure for negotiations. In the process the steady adherence to the rules provided stability to contract negotiations, a stability reflected by the elimination of the protracted strikes of the sort that had occurred in the immediate postwar period. The industry's longest strike in national negotiations after 1950 took place in 1970 when the continuation of the traditional wage rule became a bargaining issue, specifically, the continuation of the uncapped COLA formula. This is not to say that the wage formulas and continuity in fringe benefit determination eliminated all disagreements between labor and management over the exact terms of the compensation package, nor did these rules remove the occasional outbreak of strikes when impasses were reached in these negotiations.

The wage and fringe benefit rules also were attractive because they provided political stability to labor and management leaders. For the national UAW leadership, steady adherence to wage rules served an important political function by providing a standard of good performance in bargaining; the rank and file could not fault the leadership for securing wage increases that continued to satisfy the rule. This political function was particularly important in the immediate postwar environment in the face of the leadership battles underway within the UAW. The same motive held for corporate negotiators who were searching for ways to convince higher management that they were truly performing well in labor negotiations.

The importance of these political functions arises from the fact that the negotiation of a collective bargaining agreement by two opposing sides creates a bilateral monopoly and eliminates the determination of wages strictly through market forces. As a result labor and management have a degree of flexibility regarding what wage level they agree to in any given negotiation. In effect the presence of bilateral monopoly creates a zone of indeterminancy, which gives the parties some flexibility in their negotiations. Yet the existence of this indeterminancy also is the source of the political problems faced by the negotiators, for the absence of strict market determination of wages puts pressure on the negotiating parties to justify the negotiated outcomes to their membership and any higher authorities. There are always some parties sitting on the sidelines (often political rivals) who can challenge any negotiated outcome and argue that more was attainable. Hence the need for a standard of good performance in bargaining, a need well satisfied by the wage rule (Katz and Sabel 1979).

Wage rules also serve an important economic function for both labor and management by reducing the likelihood that overt conflict such as a strike will break out in the face of an impasse in negotiations. Both parties have an interest in avoiding strikes since they impose a cost of forgone income (profits or wages) on both sides. (Strikes are what economists call pareto inferior outcomes since their avoidance creates a potential joint gain.)

By providing stability and regularity to wage settlements, wage rules reduce the likelihood that negotiations will end in an impasse and reduce the range of issues over which the parties might disagree. The possibility and occurrence of disagreement is not eliminated by the use of a wage rule, but it is greatly reduced. This stability is particularly important to auto management who, in view of the long lead times associated with product development, are anxious to acquire predictability in their planning processes (Cushman 1961; Kochan and Cappelli 1984).

Connective Bargaining

Another important aspect of wage determination in the auto industry in the postwar period was the standardization of hourly wages across the Big Three. It is the breakdown of strict wage standardization that emerges as one of the novel features of bargaining in the auto industry after 1979.

There were two parts to wage standardization. One aspect centered around intercompany pattern bargaining whereby the wages set within the national collective bargaining agreement that any one of the Big Three had with the UAW was strictly copied in the agreements of the other two companies. A second aspect of wage standardization involved the interplant standardization of the wages paid similar jobs within a company. Both forms of pay standardization were imposed as part of a broader bargaining strategy adopted by labor and management in the industry—a connective bargaining structure. According to Ulman (1974, p. 98), connective bargaining

involves the negotiation of wages, fringes, and some work conditions between the company and one or more national unions, the latter connecting the company-wide wage settlements in an industry via pattern bargaining. Working conditions and, to a lesser degree, some pay questions are also negotiated at the plant level with local unions; and national unionists are sequentially involved in grievance handling.

History and Operation of Connective Bargaining

With the inclusion of the AIF and COLA wage formulas in all of the national collective bargaining agreements of the Big Three as of 1950, strict wage standardizations across the three companies followed as a consequence of rigid application of the formulas in subsequent national agreements. Some variation did remain across the company agreements regarding the form and administration of seniority, grievance, and other work rule procedures. But as with the use of the wage formulas, the striking aspect of contract negotiation in the postwar period is how strictly standardization was imposed in work rules across the Big Three.

Since the first labor agreements reached between the UAW and GM in 1938, pay and fringe benefit increases were set exclusively in national negotiations conducted at the company level.[11] Some work rules such as overtime administration procedures, employee transfer rights, and seniority guidelines were also set in the national contracts. Local unions negotiated plant-level agreements that supplemented the national agreements and influenced employment conditions through the administration of the national contract.

Since the local unions could not alter pay increases set in the national agreements, the scope of local bargaining was limited; plant-level labor and management could not devise trades involving both work rules and pay rates. In this way the strict use of wage formulas reinforced the connective bargaining structure. But although the local unions could not negotiate increases in wage rates or fringe benefits, there still existed potential room for the emergence of significant interplant and intercompany divergence in contract terms through the negotiation of the local agreements and the implementation of the national and local agreements. An important aspect of auto labor-management relations over the postwar period was the process by which this sort of divergence was limited.

Although local unions were not allowed to modify nationally determined hourly pay increases, there were two routes by which variation in hourly earnings could have developed in this system. One potential route was by way of piece rates, which as of the late 1930s were fairly common in the industry. The use of piece rates could have allowed hourly pay to vary as a function of the worker's pace and machine idiosyncrasies. But this potential source of wage variation disappeared as the national offices of the UAW gradually reduced the use of piece rate payments throughout the 1950s (MacDonald 1963).

A second route by which wage variation could have emerged in the bargaining system was through the administration of the job classification system. Nothing in the national UAW agreements mandated that workers within the same job classification in two different plants necessarily performed the same job tasks. Furthermore much discretion was left to the local union in the process by which an initial rate of pay was set for any new job. So variation in pay rates given to new jobs, if allowed to persist, could have led to interplant pay variation.

In the late 1940s and early 1950s differences in the rates of pay across plants in fact emerged as an important bargaining issue. The UAW quickly moved to tackle this problem by negotiating the creation of wage inequity funds and roving committees whose task was to remove such pay variation (MacDonald 1963). Another way the union limited interplant pay variation was to require national union approval of individual wage rates established on new jobs (Harbison and Dubin 1947, p. 60).

Local collective bargaining agreements in the auto industry define work rules such as the exact form of the seniority ladder, job characteristics, job bidding and transfer rights, health and safety standards, production standards, and an array of other rules that guide shop floor production. An important part of the process of contract administration is the grievance system with binding third-party arbitration serving as the end point of disputes regarding the interpretation and implementation of both the national and local contract. Any strikes that arise during the term of a local contract over any of these arbitrable issues are automatically deemed unauthorized by the national union, although, as stipulated by the national auto contracts, there is no binding arbitration for local disputes concerning production standards, new job rates, and health and safety issues. Local unions are free to address any disputes involving these issues during the term of their local contract through strike action.

Local bargaining over work rules did (and continues to) provide some room for the expression of local preferences and adjustment to local conditions. Within plants shop floor fractional bargaining of the sort described by Kuhn (1961) emerged when work groups utilized the grievance procedure or informal pressure in pursuit of their interests. Furthermore occasional unauthorized (wildcat) strikes occurred over the postwar years in which workers pressed their demands regarding shop floor working conditions.[13]

Substantial divergence in work rules and even wage rates could have emerged within this bargaining system, but it did not. Substantial standardization in contract terms was maintained through the efforts of both the national union and corporate management. A critical element in the connective bargaining structure was the active role the national offices of the UAW played in monitoring plant-level bargaining and contract administration. Their formal power came from the fact that many features of local agreements, as well as local strikes, require the approval of the national union. For example, local contract language concerning the form of the seniority ladder must be approved by the national UAW offices (Ford Motor Company, 1982a, article 8, sec. 3, p. 69). The same is true for local wage agreements and for the wage rates on new jobs. Furthermore the national union must give approval before a local strike can be authorized or before any unresolved grievance can be pushed for resolution by way of third-party arbitration (Ford Motor Company, 1982a, article 7, sec. 23(d), p. 64, sec. 8, p. 51).

The national union acquired the power to approve local agreements during the term of the 1942 GM-UAW agreement. The national union, however, was not the only party interested in centralizing the regulation of local negotiations. Corporate management also favored this centralization and may well have initially suggested to the national union that it acquire the power to approve local union actions.[14]

Over the postwar years the recourse to either foreign or domestic nonunion supply of parts previously produced in plants of the Big Three occasionally had significant employment consequences within selected plants. The pressure of employment displacement could have led to local work rule modifications and interplant divergence as part of an effort to lower in-house costs (in Big Three plants) so as to compete more effectively with alternative suppliers. Levinson (1960) reports that unionized supplier plants outside the Big Three periodically faced competitive pressure from lower-cost firms and responded to such competition by reducing their pay levels and modifying work rules so that their own contract terms less closely followed those in the Big Three. But this sort of contract modification did not occur to a significant degree within the Big Three until the emergence of such contract modifications after 1979.

Through the spread of the Big Three pattern to the independent companies in the 1950s and American Motors after 1961, additional standardization in contract terms was maintained in the auto industry. In the early 1950s a few small car companies remained in the industry: Nash-Kelvinator, Studebaker-Packard, Kaiser-Willys, and Hudson Motor Company. The pay rates and other contract terms in these companies were close to those in the Big Three, and any significant differences typically involved the provision of above-pattern terms in the independent companies (MacDonald 1963, chap. 6; Edwards 1965, pp. 116–117). Finding it difficult to compete with the scale efficiencies attained by the larger Big Three producers, these independent companies repeatedly faced financial difficulties during the 1950s. The independents appealed to the UAW for modifications in their contract terms, and occasionally the union agreed to changes in pay rates and work rules. On the whole, however, the UAW was unwilling to allow the contract terms in any of the independent companies to diverge significantly from the terms within the Big Three even when those companies faced imminent bankruptcy.

The same resistance to pattern breaking held in the UAW's relationship with American Motors (AMC) formed in 1954 by a merger of two of the independents, Nash-Kelvinator and Hudson Motors (MacDonald 1963, pp. 291–306). AMC did negotiate the addition of a profit-sharing plan in 1961, a marked departure from the wage rules in the Big Three agreements, but this plan never generated any sizable pay increases. When AMC faced financial problems repeatedly in the 1970s, it negotiated contracts with the UAW that included slight deviations from the Big Three pattern settlements. In the AMC agreements wage increases took the same form as the Big Three formula-generated increases, but the AMC wage increases and adoption of fringe benefit improvements typically lagged the Big Three pattern settlement by a year (Bureau of National Affairs, various years). In the process the standardization of contract terms was extended to the independent companies, as well as across the Big Three companies.

Economic Functions of Connective Bargaining
Why did the parties favor both intercompany and intracompany standardization in pay and work rules? As with the wage rules, the answer lies in the functions served by this procedure. The national union was particularly interested in the standardization of contract terms across plants and companies because it prevented management from shifting production to plants or companies with lower costs (Chamberlain 1961). The substitution of low-cost labor would have

greatly reduced the union's ability to bargain for higher pay and better work conditions.

The possibility of intracompany shifts in production as a device to undercut the union arose from the fact that in the late 1940s, southern auto plants apparently had tighter production standards and lower pay rates. Having won representation rights in all of the Big Three plants and armed with a union security clause, the UAW was well positioned to limit management's ability to shift production to unorganized plants. Yet if intrafirm wage and work rule variation was allowed, management could shift production to plants with the lowest production costs. Furthermore if intercompany differences in employment conditions were allowed to become significant competitive factors, the union would face pressure to lower employment standards to the lowest common denominator. Standardization of contract terms within and across companies limited management's ability to whipsaw the union in this fashion.

Two environmental economic factors contributed to the union's reluctance to allow intracompany divergence in contract terms. First, the industry's output and employment was on an upward long-run growth path. Consequently any business lost to an outside supplier due to the union's opposition to the lowering of in-house wages or employment standards was most often made up for by an expanding volume of business activities left in-house. And if volume expansion was not sufficient to avoid layoffs within a given plant, liberal transfer rights and moving allowances provided in the union's national contract allowed workers displaced in one plant to bid on new jobs in other plants covered by the national agreement. As a result, and in contrast to the recent period, local unions were not under pressure to make major modifications to work rules in order to save jobs.

The union's reluctance to allow company exceptions to the dominant pattern was also motivated by economic factors in the auto market. In the 1950s and 1960s the level of imports into the U.S. automobile market was extremely small: 0.8 percent of total domestic car sales in 1955 and 6.1 percent in 1965 (MVMA 1981, p. 13). Consequently any sales lost by a failing independent company were most likely picked up by another domestic company.

The union faced extremely inelastic demand for labor because it organized the entire U.S. auto industry and the industry faced little competition from foreign producers. Any lowering of labor costs in a single company would exert little effect on total employment in the industry or on union membership. In fact until the late 1970s the pressure on the union for intercompany contract divergence was even weaker than that existing for intracompany divergence because, at least with regard to the outsourcing of parts production, there was a viable threat that business lost from the Big Three firms might shift to workplaces not organized by the UAW.

Thus given the limited penetration of imports into the domestic auto market, the national coverage of the company agreements, and the union security provisions included in those agreements, there was a match between the relevant product and labor markets until the late 1970s.[15] This match greatly enhanced the UAW's bargaining power while contributing to the union's attraction to connective bargaining.

Political Functions of Connective Bargaining
Another important pressure for standardization in pay and work rules came from the fact that standardization satisfied the work forces' equity concerns. It appears that workers (and probably everyone else) are not primarily driven by the desire to receive ever higher compensation and consequently do not possess absolute wants (Ross 1948). Rather workers are motivated most strongly by the desire to maintain their relative position with critical reference groups. In this way orbits of coercive comparison come to play an important role in wage determination, thus encouraging the practice of pay standardization.

One way to explain the origin of these relativistic demands is to view them as a product of the indeterminancy that arises from the bilateral power relationship between labor and management. This indeterminancy gives the parties room in their negotiation of employment conditions and leaves them searching for guideposts or reference points that will signal when an adequate job within bargaining has been attained. In this view the autoworkers' concern for comparability in work conditions arises from the same pressure as does the use of wage rules. In wage setting, I argued earlier, the negotiating parties resort to wage rules as both a guidepost and a way to answer rival parties who might otherwise complain that an inadequate settlement was reached. Workers' desire for comparability in work terms across plants can be explained in an analogous manner where comparability serves a similar guidepost function and resolves workers' doubts as to whether an adequate bargain has been fashioned.

With pay increases set at the national level, this labor relations system did not provide any direct connection between the determination of pay and local work rules. The system was still connective, however, due to the fact that the national union was heavily involved in monitoring local union affairs and functioned as a channel of communication up and down the union hierarchy particularly through its involvement in the administration of the grievance procedure and by way of the pattern following that standardized employment conditions within and across the companies.

This process shifted political power inside the UAW to the national union officers. In this way the imposition of the connective bargaining structure in the immediate postwar years was associated with the rise and solidification of the Reuther faction within the UAW (Lichtenstein 1982). The elaboration of the connective structure in the autoworkers' union in the late 1940s and early 1950s also paralleled a similar centralization underway in national unions throughout U.S. industry (Weber 1961).

Management, on the other hand, was in favor of the national union's exercising firmer control over the local plants because once the possibility of shifting production as a way to lower costs was diminished, the possibility loomed that the union would use interplant variation as a device to whipsaw management into better and better work conditions. This could have occurred if, after having won a particularly favorable item in one plant, the union was able to use this victory to rally workers to demand a similar item in other plants (Harbison and Dubin 1947, pp. 61–62). In addition the centralization of power into the hands of Reuther and other national UAW leaders provided by the connective bargaining structure had some clear advantages for auto management by limiting the influence of radical local unions or leaders (Lichtenstein 1982). Furthermore the steady upward growth in auto sales and limited penetration of imports helped keep management content with the connective bargaining structure, just at it had for the union.

By producing a separation between work rule bargaining and compensation determination, this connective structure also served to discourage the creation of a broader cost awareness among workers, an awareness that might have led workers to concern themselves with business decision making. However, workers' involvement in broad business decision making would have violated another of the key features of the auto labor relations system, its job control focus.

Job Control

Operation of Job Control Unionism
There are three basic characteristics of labor-management relations in the auto industry producing a job control focus.[16] First, the labor relations system relies heavily on formal, written, and legalistic procedures. The collective bargaining agreements between the UAW and the companies are voluminous and specify employment terms and conditions in fine detail. The operation of the grievance procedure with its formal four steps in which higher levels of management and

the union are called in to settle a dispute and quasi-judicial opinions are issued by third-party arbitrators contributes to the legalistic and formal nature of the system.[17]

A second aspect of the job control orientation in U.S. auto labor relations is the large role played by the detailed job classification system, which includes specification of the exact requirements of each job. The job classifications described in the chart reproduced in figure 2.4 represent part of the twelve charts that make up the seniority bumping ladder in one auto plant's local agreement. These detailed job classifications are the basic ingredients of the complicated seniority bumping rights, shift preferences, and other job rights regulated by the national and local contractual agreements. An important feature of the job classification system is the fact that wages are tied to each classification, not to the worker.[18]

A third defining attribute of the job control system is the limited involvement of workers in production or business decision making. Clearly, through collective bargaining, workers and the UAW significantly affect employment conditions. Yet the autoworker has

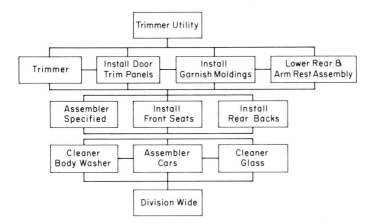

Figure 2.4
Example of seniority ladder. Source: General Motors Corporation (1976).

little, if any, involvement in ongoing production decisions. As the autoworkers aptly describe the system, it is one where management pays for the workers' hands but is not interested in use of the workers' minds.[19]

Use of the term *job control unionism* as a characterization of the auto bargaining system is not intended to be synonymous with the expression *business unionism*, a term used by Hoxie (1920) and others to characterize the U.S labor relations system. The term *business unionism* conveys a union's political platform and refers to labor's general acceptance of the capitalist system and rejection of a more radical and broader political platform. *Job control unionism* refers to the particular form of union participation in decision making and the scope of that participation. Although the UAW's job control focus is strongly supported by and consistent with the union's business unionist philosophy, it is possible for a union to follow business unionism and not be job control oriented. The labor unions in Japan's auto industry are examples.

History of Job Control Unionism
Auto management's efforts to limit the scope of collective bargaining had begun with the union's first success at organization and had continued vigorously during World War II. In its first negotiations with the UAW, auto management pushed for (and largely got) collective bargaining agreements that preserved managerial prerogatives and limited workers' and the union's involvement in business decisions. During the war GM management worked hard to keep its relationship with the union at arms length (Harbison and Dubin 1947, p. 51). Worry that the union and workers might gain greater influence over production issues led GM management during the war to refuse to participate in government-sponsored production committees. Furthermore during this period and after the war, GM management led the campaign for the preservation of strict limits on the arbitration system and forcefully opposed any form of joint administration out-

side of a narrow set of issues (Harbison and Dubin 1947, p. 46; Harris 1982; Lichtenstein 1982).

Even in the Studebaker Corporation, where labor and management had forged a more cooperative relationship in the 1940s and early 1950s, there was no broadening of the collective bargaining agenda. There, as in the rest of the industry, the union remained a party that bargained for better pay and work conditions but was not counseled regarding or allowed to participate in broader business decisions (Harbison and Dubin 1947, p. 204).

Support for these narrow bounds in collective bargaining came during World War II from the National War Labor Board. The board emphasized the need for management to formalize and regularize personnel administration. At the same time the board encouraged the development of sharp limits on the authority of third-party arbitration by exempting business decisions from the procedure. Rather the board emphasized management's right to change work rules without the prior consent of the union and in this way push what became a basic principle in U.S. labor relations: management's right to move and the union's right to then grieve any moves it did not like (Harris 1982, p. 55).[20]

The dominance of a job control focus did not lead to a complete stabilization of shop floor labor-management relations. Labor and management often engaged in struggles over the exact terms of working conditions and the bounds of union or worker involvement in decision making. Frequently these issues were addressed through informal day-to-day relations between workers and their supervisors, but occasionally disputes produced either authorized or unauthorized local strike actions.

In addition the combination of connective bargaining and job control unionism did not produce standardization in the tenor or outputs of shop floor labor relations because the focus of connective bargaining was on standardizing contractual terms. Meanwhile job control unionism produced adversarial and formal labor-management relations. Significant variation emerged in the tenor and practical conduct of shop floor labor-management relations across plants and across work groups within given plants. In some plants there was a constant acrimonious relationship, while in others the parties developed a more cooperative relationship. The wide diversity in shop floor relations is revealed by the variation in plant-level industrial relations performance indicators from two GM divisions. For example, the grievance rate in a given division and year varies by a factor of 20, and the absentee rate is twice as high in one plant as it is in another.

Eras in Labor-Management Relations
The intensity and scope of shop floor labor-management relations also varied significantly over time in the postwar period; however, in broad terms it is possible to trace some patterns in these relations. In the prewar and war years the initiative for workplace bargaining lay in the hands of the UAW, strengthened by the spread of union representation. By the late 1940s and 1950s that initiative had shifted to management, a shift that occurred not only in the auto industry but characterized many other organized industries (Harris 1982; Strauss 1962). The late 1940s and 1950s can be characterized as an era of managerial initiatives where auto management tried hard to limit (and in many instances succeeded) the influence of workers and the UAW on what were deemed to be key managerial prerogatives such as production standards (Herding 1972; Lichtenstein 1982). Nonetheless the presence of this managerial offensive did not foreclose the UAW's success at regularizing its influence over many workplace issues during the late 1940s and 1950s.

The economic expansion of the mid- and late 1960s and the social changes underway broadly in American society led to a new era in auto bargaining from the mid-1960s through the early 1970s.[21] This era was marked by shop floor militance and local strike waves (*Busi-*

ness Week 1964; Serrin 1973; Rothchild 1973). Reflecting this rise in shop floor militance, the number of written grievances per 100 blue-collar employees in the plants covered by the GM-UAW national agreement rose from 50.4 in 1960 to 71.9 in 1973.[22] Heightened shop floor militance also led to more contentious and difficult local contract negotiations. For example, the number of union demands submitted in local contract negotiations in General Motors rose from 11,000 in 1958 to 39,200 in 1973.

Shop floor militance also led to more frequent and intense local strikes. The percentage of total working time lost in work stoppages in the motor vehicle and equipment industry varied between 0.21 and 0.28 in those years between 1959 and 1963 when a new national contract was not being negotiated. In 1968 and 1969 (also noncontract years) the percentage of days lost rose, respectively, to 0.74 and 0.94 (U.S. Department of Labor 1979b). In February 1972 a strike that occurred at the GM-Lordstown plant came to symbolize this era of worker militance (Rothchild 1973).

In this era both management and the UAW national leadership were struggling to reassert the more disciplined regularity that had characterized shop floor labor relations in the 1950s. This led Walter Reuther in some instances to guide the settlement of local contract negotiations and not allow local strikes (Selekman 1964, pp. 551, 552).

To some extent it was inevitable that there would be a tension between the national and local unions regarding the extent of each's influence. The important fact about the challenges that did emerge to national union control over the postwar period is that these challenges were accommodated through adjustment in the existing connective bargaining structure and until the recent period did not produce major modification of the connective bargaining structure.

High rates of absenteeism, production slowdowns, and the unsettled nature of shop floor labor relations also led auto management in the late 1960s to search for alternative approaches to worker-supervisor relations and new motivational tools. QWL programs developed in part to respond to this wave of shop floor militance and improve the tenor of labor-management relations in the plants that perennially were relatively poor performers. In their early years QWL programs were viewed as supplements to the existing job control system and to be kept separate from other collective bargaining procedures. As a result, although the QWL programs emerged as an important innovation within auto labor relations, the new programs, like the challenges by local unions to national union control, were accommodated through amendments to the existing labor relations system and were not fundamental alterations in the basic structure of the system.

Functions of Job Control Unionism
A number of factors explain why job control unionism was adopted in the U.S. auto labor relations system. For management the job control focus served the important function of containing the union's and worker's penetration of issues deemed to be managerial prerogatives. As Harbison and Dubin note, containment of the union was a central objective for auto management in the postwar period (Harbison and Dubin, 1974, pp. 48–88). The labor relations system that emerged largely resolved this concern by limiting the bargaining agenda. Furthermore job control unionism meshed well with management's adherence to scientific management, which professed the advantages of supervisory authority and a clear definition of workers' responsibilities (Piore 1982; Piore and Sabel 1984).

For the UAW, although the limited bargaining agenda did not satisfy all of Reuther's initial goals, this system did produce satisfactory outcomes. Job control unionism helped to bring about a production system that generated high rates of growth in autoworkers' real compensation and long-run growth in employment.

The limited bounds of collective bargaining also were consistent with the business unionist tradition in the U.S. labor movement (Hoxie

1920). The dominance of the AFL in the early twentieth century and a number of other factors had helped to create in American labor an acceptance of private property and a general acceptance of the capitalist system. Labor's limited involvement in business decision making was highly compatible with this political framework and its voluntarist traditions.

U.S. labor's business unionism and broad acceptance of the capitalist system did not preclude the emergence of adversarial relations on the shop floor. The central element of this adversarial pattern is the low trust with which labor and management view each other. From labor's side a lack of trust in management in part springs from the ever-present fear that management will use any available opportunity to remove the union from the plant. On management's side the low trust seems to arise from the fear that labor will utilize its representation rights and bargaining power to press unwarranted and damaging demands. Nonetheless, in the presence of low-trust relations, it makes sense for both sides to seek protection in the legalistic and formal adjudication of disputes and work rules (Fox 1974). By regulating work conditions through legalistic documents and focusing their fights over narrow interpretations of the terms of the collective bargaining agreement, both sides were protected from the possibility that more free-for-all bargaining would jeopardize their security. In that way job control unionism was very compatible with business and adversarial unionism.

Another reason why job control unionism flourished in the auto industry is because as a key feature of the labor relations system, it meshed well with other parts of the auto labor relations system. During negotiations over wages adherence to the wage rules led the parties away from any discussion of either company profits or prices. For example, why should the parties discuss corporate profits since whether profits were drifting up or down had little impact on either wage changes or the negotiated fringe benefit package? Nor was there much reason for negotiators to debate broad corporate concerns such as investment planning, parts outsourcing, and problems associated with the introduction of new technologies. Keeping the union and negotiations away from concern for either prices or profits was an explicit motivation for the adoption of the wage rules when GM management was searching for a way to answer and avoid Walter Reuther's early requests to discuss those issues.

At the local level the job control focus similarly discouraged worker involvement in business and production decision making. The resolution of disagreements through the grievance procedure and the reliance on the detailed local contract as a guide to worker responsibilities left little room for alternative forms of worker participation in decision making.

Summary

Various shifts and strains in labor-management relations across plants and time in the auto industry exercised a critical influence on work conditions and the balance of power between labor and management. At the same time the three key features of the auto industry's labor relations system provided a structure that bounded and stabilized shop floor bargaining. In particular the importance of the wage and fringe benefit rules and the job control focus produced sharp limits on the extent of worker and union involvement in business decisions. Meanwhile connective bargaining placed limits on the role of local union and shop floor actions.

The three features of the auto labor relations system—wage rules, connective bargaining, and job control—thereby historically have been linked into a highly centralized labor relations system. Wages are set at the national level, and local work rule bargaining occurs within limits imposed by the national union. Furthermore union and worker participation in business decisions is limited, formalized, and contractually based.

From the late 1940s until the late 1970s this labor relations system produced steadily rising real compensation to autoworkers and long-term growth in auto employment and production. With limited import penetration in auto sales, this was a bargaining system where the geographic bounds of union organization closely matched the relevant product market. The consistency the labor relations system had with the economic environment was one of the primary factors contributing to the system's attractiveness to both labor and management. The auto bargaining system also served important political functions for labor and management by providing stability and continuity in negotiation processes.

Periodic amendments were made to the labor relations system's three key features between 1948 and 1979 in response to problems, but these amendments did not fundamentally alter the basic operation of the system. The unique aspect of auto bargaining between 1979 and 1983 was the extent to which changes were made to the auto collective bargaining system that went beyond mere amendment of the system.

Changes Made to the
Wage Rules, Local Work
Rules, and Connective
Bargaining after 1979

One of the sustaining features of the auto collective bargaining system in the post–World War II years was the consistency of the outputs of that system with the economic environment. Consequently when the U.S. auto industry went into an unprecedented economic slump from 1979 until mid-1983, the viability of the bargaining system that had been operating for thirty years was called into question. Heightened international competition and greater volatility and uncertainty in market demand created the need for cost reduction and greater flexibility in the allocation of human resources. This led to changes in each of the three key features of the auto collective bargaining system. These changes were first perceived by labor and management as amendments to the bargaining system, which like earlier amendments would not require more fundamental alterations. A close examination, however, reveals that the changes adopted after 1979, individually and through their cumulative effects, caused an erosion of the basic bargaining system that has traditionally operated in the auto industry.

The Economic Slump

There are many indicators of the scope of the industry's decline. The employment of production workers in the auto industry (SIC 371) dropped from a peak of 800,800 in December 1978 to a low of 487,700 in January 1983 (Department of Labor, various years). The number of autoworkers on indefinite layoff from the Big Three went as high as 247,000 in August 1980, substantially surpassing the layoff peaks in any of the previous postwar recessions (Ward's 1980). Unemployment rates in communities whose economic base was founded on the auto industry rose to depression levels.[1] Meanwhile the combined dollar losses of the Big Three were $4.0 billion in 1980 and $1.2 billion in 1981 (Standard and Poors).

The layoffs and prolonged unemployment that followed after 1979 had a harsher effect on autoworkers than earlier downturns in the industry because of the social welfare policies of the Reagan administration. In the mid- and late 1970s trade adjustment assistance (TAA) benefits had become a significant source of income support for autoworkers laid off during the industry's downturns in the 1974–1975 sales slump and the early stages of the 1979–1983 slump. An estimated 685,066 laid-off autoworkers received roughly $2.2 billion of the total $3.0 billion in TAA benefits provided between 1975 and 1981.[2] After 1981, however, TAA benefits and eligibility were greatly reduced.

The Reagan-backed appropriations bill for 1982 sharply cut back the TAA program; it tightened eligibility standards and curtailed federal extensions of state unemployment insurance benefits. At one point these federal extensions had provided up to an additional thirty-nine weeks of benefits beyond the unemployment benefits in state programs (typically a maximum of twenty-six weeks). For the unemployed in Michigan federal 1982 appropriations legislation eliminated thirteen weeks of extended unemployment benefits. (These extensions later were reinstated in 1983 by congressional authorization.)

Although the depth of the decline in auto sales was enormous, its most unusual aspect was its length. The industry had experienced sharp cyclical flux over the postwar period as illustrated in the fluctuations in employment reported earlier in figure 2.1 and had made necessary adjustments. Management had adjusted inventory and purchasing policies to cope with cyclical flux. On the labor relations front contractual recall and layoff rights and the SUB system had been created to respond to cyclical flux in employment levels.

But neither labor nor management was accustomed to or prepared for the prolonged decline in sales that started in 1979. As the slump deepened, the SUB funds were run down, and SUB payments were cut back. Hopes of recall diminished as many laid-off autoworkers exceeded the year-long recall rights allowed in the national UAW contracts. Given the heavy concentration of auto production in north-central states and a deep recession in the national economy, many laid-off autoworkers were forced to relocate to the South or West in search of employment opportunities. For the auto companies the prolonged nature of the sales slump and the attendant financial losses raised doubts about their capital-raising capacity and their future economic viability.

The 1979–1983 sales decline acquired even greater significance because it appeared to signal a fundamental deterioration in the competitive position of the U.S. producers in the world auto market. What was at issue was not an extremely deep cyclical decline, although cyclical factors clearly played a role in the sales decline. Rather the industry appeared to be undergoing a more fundamental transformation. One indicator of this transformation was the rise in the share of the domestic market going to imported cars and trucks from 14.6 percent in 1970 to 25.2 percent in 1981.[3]

Another indicator of altered competitive relations in the world auto market was the emergence of a significant cost differential between U.S. and Japanese producers. Some analysts argue that the differential is a high as $2,000 for a standard subcompact car (Altshuler et al. 1984; Abernathy, Clark, and Kantrow 1983). Consideration of product quality (especially fit and trim) put the U.S. producers even further behind their Japanese competitors. The exact dimensions of the cost and quality differentials are extremely difficult, if not impossible, to measure due to differences in product mix, industry structure, and compensation structure in the two countries. It is my view that we do not yet know the size of the differential, but its exact dimensions were unimportant.

The important fact was that the sales slump created pressure on labor and management to search for changes in labor relations that would help the industry's recovery. In addition to the enormous sales slump, labor and management were searching for new labor relations practices that would respond to the possibility that the postwar dominance of the U.S. auto industry and the rapid long-run growth characterizing auto sales from 1946 until 1979 were over.[4] It was that possibility that made the recent sales downturn so different from earlier cyclical downturns.

Broad Implications of the Economic Slump for Labor Relations

The U.S. auto industry came under pressure to lower costs both as a way to respond to foreign competition and as a method to stimulate overall motor vehicle demand. The pressure to lower labor costs was enhanced by relative wage comparisons like those in table 3.1 that show that U.S. autoworkers earn higher wages than autoworkers in foreign countries.

Table 3.1
Hourly compensation costs for production workers in motor vehicles and equipment industry, 1975 and 1981

	1975		1981	
	U.S. Dollars	Index (U.S. = 100)	U.S. Dollars	Index (U.S. = 100)
United States	9.44	100	17.55	100
West Germany	7.68	81	12.89	73
Sweden	7.44	79	11.50	66
France	5.22	55	9.20	52
Italy	5.10	54	7.86	45
United Kingdom	3.96	42	7.83	45
Japan	3.56	38	7.74	44

Source: U.S. Department of Labor (1983a).
Note: These figures include assessment of the cost of fringe benefits as well as wages, bonuses, and deferred compensation. The figures cover the industry as a whole and not just the main assemblers, though the degree of vertical integration covered is not identical in each country.

Table 3.1 reports hourly compensation costs for production workers in the motor vehicle industries of the major producing nations in 1975 and 1981. These figures include a standardized assessment of fringe benefit costs and the costs of wage payments. The figures are expressed in U.S. dollar equivalents and thereby are affected by exchange rates. It is virtually impossible to derive a full comparative assessment of all fringe benefits and completely standardize for the degree of vertical integration in each national auto industry. Nonetheless these figures provide a good approximate comparison of wage costs.[5] The figures show that U.S. autoworkers receive hourly wages that are significantly higher than workers in all other major producing countries.

Two different labor relations strategies emerged out of the effort to lower costs. One approach was to try to lower production costs directly through compensation reductions or changes in work practices that effectively increase labor effort per dollar of compensation. Another approach to labor relations reform was to seek efficiency gains through better cooperation between labor and management either within the existing system or through a restructuring of the labor relations system. The goal here was to assist the industry's recovery by creating joint gains and lowering production costs in ways that were not at labor's expense.

After 1979 the industry began to pursue these routes in an effort to lower costs and gain enhanced flexibility. In the process the three key features of the labor relations system were significantly modified.

Wage Rules

Negotiations at Chrysler
The wage rules traditionally used to set pay levels were modified first as part of efforts to avoid the bankruptcy of the Chrysler Corporation in 1979 and then in contractual agreements reached at GM and Ford in the spring of 1982. After reporting record losses, Chrysler manage-

ment entered national contract negotiations in the fall of 1979 insist-
ing that union concessions, as well loan guarantees from federal,
state, and local governments, were necessary for the company's sur-
vival.[6] Chrysler and the UAW proceeded to negotiate an agreement
that deviated substantially from the pattern settlements reached at
Ford and GM in September 1979. The 1979–1982 national contracts
at Ford and GM had continued the use of the traditional COLA and
AIF wage formulas and provided a number of fringe benefit improvements, including an increase in the number of paid personal
holidays.[7]

The contract signed by Chrysler and the UAW in October 1979 provided $203 million in wage concessions over its term. The three-year
agreement maintained the formula wage mechanisms but deferred
payment of the scheduled COLA and AIF increases. The COLA increases were to be paid a quarter later than usual, and the AIF 3
percent increases were deferred for six, four, and two months in each
of the successive contract years. Other concessions included pension
increases equal to about 70 percent of those negotiated at GM and
Ford, no increase in sickness and accident benefits, and no paid personal holidays in the first year and six fewer over term. As part of the
contract settlement, Chrsyler agreed to nominate UAW President
Douglas Fraser for a seat on the company's board of directors.

Before adjourning on December 21, 1979, Congress passed a $3.5
billion aid package guaranteeing $1.5 billion in federal loans to Chrys-
ler while also setting the following targets for contributions from
other sources to aid Chrysler's recovery: $462.5 million in union
wage-benefit concessions; $125 million in concessions from salaried
Chrysler employees; $500 million in loans from U.S. banks; $150 million in loans from foreign (mostly Canadian) banks; $300 million from
the sale of Chrysler assets; $180 million from suppliers; $50 million
from the sale of new Chrysler stock; and $250 million from state,
local, and foreign governments.

In response to Congress's request for further concessions, the UAW and Chrysler returned to the bargaining table and negotiated a further $243 million in wage and benefit reductions in January 1980. In this second round of concessions the scheduled AIF increases were deferred an additional two months in the second contract year and three and a half months in the third contract year. The parties also agreed to reduce the number of paid personal holidays to three over the term of the contract, and the company agreed to establish an employee stock ownership plan. The agreement contained a clause stipulating that at the end of the term of the contract (before its renegotiation in September 1982), the traditional COLA and AIF formulas would be fully reinstated, and all fringe benefits at Chrysler were to be improved so as to match those in place at Ford and GM.

Chrysler, however, continued to face financial difficulties throughout 1980, and under the threat of imminent bankruptcy labor and management returned to the bargaining table a third time. In January 1981 Chrysler and the UAW agreed to a further $156 million in pay concessions. This time the scheduled 3 percent AIF increases for 1981 and 1982 were cancelled. In addition COLA payments for 1979 to 1981, previously accruing, ceased, as did further scheduled COLA increases for the duration of the contract. These concessions provided the effective elimination of COLA and AIF formula wage increases over the 1979–1982 term of the contract. The total effect of all of the compensation concessions negotiated at Chrysler was to lower the hourly pay of Chrysler workers approximately $2.50 below the pay received by workers at Ford and GM by the end of the agreement.[8]

GM and Ford Negotiations
An enormous and sustained decline in sales led to large layoffs and a significant number of plant closings at Ford and GM in 1980 and 1981.[9] This led to the negotiation of new contracts at these companies in March 1982 prior to the scheduled expiration date of September 1982 in the then-existing 1979–1982 national agreements.[10]

As at Chrysler, the compensation concessions agreed to at Ford and GM included major modification of the traditional wage rules. The Ford and GM agreements eliminated the AIF increases scheduled for 1982 and 1983. Three quarterly COLA increases were deferred for eighteen months, though after December 1982, regular COLA increases of 1 cent per 0.26 point increase in the consumer price index continued. Additionally all paid personal holidays (nine per year in the 1979–1982 agreement) and one regular holiday were eliminated. The net effect of the elimination of the holidays was to raise annual work hours 4 percent. The new contracts included profit-sharing plans. At Ford the profit-sharing plan took effect on January 1, 1983, and provided workers with a share of profits whenever before-tax profits exceeded 2.3 percent of total sales by U.S. Ford operations. The formula calls for workers to share 10 percent of profits between 2.3 and 4.6 percent, 12.5 percent of those between 4.6 and 6.9 percent, and 15 percent of all profits in excess of 6.9 percent. Had the plan been in effect in the 1970s, it would have generated annual payouts between $117 and $505 to Ford workers.[11] The GM profit-sharing plan was similar in its terms. The 1982 contracts also included a clause providing for the opening and renegotiation of the terms of the agreement after January 1, 1983, if auto sales were to improve significantly.

The contracts at Ford and GM included a number of new programs that improved the income and job security of autoworkers. Under a new guaranteed income stream benefit program, permanently laid-off workers with more than fifteen years seniority will receive 50 percent of their last year's earnings (and an additional 1 percent for each year of seniority beyond fifteen up to a maximum of 75 percent of last years pay) until reaching normal retirement age.[12] A joint national employee development and training program at each company funded by company contributions (10 cents per worker hour at GM) also was created to provide counseling, training, and tuition assistance to laid-off and employed workers.[13]

The 1982 agreements provided for the initiation of experiments with employment guarantees at select plants (four at GM and three at Ford). In these plants 80 percent of the existing work force would be guaranteed employment during the term of the agreement (until September 1984).[14] In addition management promised not to close any plants for twenty-four months "as a result of outsourcing the components manufactured in the facility," although plant closings would be permitted for volume-related reasons or as a consequence of internal company consolidations of operations. The companies also pledged to try to maintain existing employment levels and employ their best efforts to replace jobs lost by outsourcing. The companies made lump sum contributions to the SUB funds, which had become sorely depleted, and made it possible for workers with more than ten years of seniority to receive up to 104 weeks of SUB pay. The new guaranteed income stream program, plant closing moratorium, SUB funds, and related contractual changes were announced as the job security components of the new contracts.

The job security measures included in the 1982 GM and Ford agreements served two purposes. On the one hand, the new programs function as partial compensation to the union and autoworkers for the pay concessions. The job security measures also appear to serve a symbolic function by providing some direct assurances to the workers that the pay concessions will in fact lead to an improvement in their job security. One could argue that by reducing their compensation, autoworkers improved the cost competitiveness of U.S. cars and UAW labor on the international market, which will lead to an increase in vehicle sales and employment. It is not clear that the companies' pledge not to close any additional plants for twenty-four months because of component outsourcing will induce either GM or Ford to do something they would not otherwise have done in the face of the pay concessions agreed to in the 1982 contract, which on their own reduce the economic incentive for outsourcing. However, the inclusion of the plant closing moratorium made the gain in job security explicit and enabled the union leadership to show workers that something was won in exchange for the pay concessions. It appears that this sort of explicit linking of concessions and employment enhancement is often necessary to convince workers of the value of such concessions.

The new national contracts also created mutual growth forums at both national and local levels where labor and management would meet to discuss "business developments that are of material interest and significance to the union, the employees, and the company."[15] Furthermore the contracts provided that the national directors of the respective UAW Ford and GM departments would be able to address the companies' board of directors twice yearly.[16]

Although the concessionary agreements included a number of new programs and changes in scheduled wage increases, throughout the process of pay modification, labor and management pursued a course that maintained the structure of the traditional wage rules. The pattern was first to delay the implementation of wage-rule-generated increases and only after more severe pressure to cancel those pay increases. Note, for example, that the concessionary agreements at Chrysler provided for the later full restoration of the traditional AIF and COLA formulas, and the 1982 agreements at GM and Ford provided for full restoration of the traditional COLA formula prior to the expiration of the contracts. This allowed union leaders to claim that these formulas had not been abandoned but only temporarily deferred.

Fringe Benefit Concessions
With respect to fringe benefits, the changes at the Big Three also followed a very structured pattern. The major adjustment made to fringe benefits in the Chrysler agreements and the 1982 Ford and GM agreements was elimination of paid personal holidays. The inclusion of paid personal holidays into the autoworkers' contracts first had

occurred in the 1976 agreements. Consequently the paid personal holidays represented the latest major extension of the autoworkers' fringe benefit package.

By eliminating these holidays, the parties pursued a course that least disrupted the basic structure of the fringe package. An alternative course would have been to arrive at comparable labor cost savings by modifying a number of the fringe benefits. For example, for years management had been trying to modify the health insurance plan so as to require copayment by autoworkers. Cost savings from the fringe benefit package could have been derived through this and other minor changes to other fringe benefits, but modifications were not made in this fashion.

Part of the explanation for this behavior seems to lie in the fact that the fringe benefits arise from long campaigns by the UAW. Once included in the agreement, these benefits then acquire standing as an entitlement or principle. Thus when economic pressure forced a reduction in the benefit package, it occurred through elimination of the latest fringe benefit added to the package and not through a less targeted approach.[17]

For senior workers not affected by any net employment decline produced by the lengthening of work hours, the elimination of paid personal holidays did not lead to any change in total annual income. Therefore reduction of the fringe benefit package in this manner also may reflect the interests of senior autoworkers in preserving their annual income levels.

The total net effect of the wage and fringe benefit concessions is to reduce the rise in total hourly labor costs in GM and Ford after March 1982 from the approximately $5.50 it would have been in the absence of the concessions to an actual rise of approximately $3.50 by September 1984.

Profit Sharing
One of the ways the basic wage system was amended at Chrysler,
Ford, and GM in these negotiations was through the introduction of
profit-sharing plans. These programs are a form of contingent compensation in that they tie autoworkers' earnings to the economic performance of the firms. With this contingency property, profit sharing
has wider implications in addition to the fact that it produces earnings
that are less certain from the workers' viewpoint. By linking compensation to company performance, the profit-sharing plans remove the
traditional strict interfirm pattern following that characterized pay
setting since 1950. If the economic performance of Ford and GM were
to diverge, then with profit sharing, autoworkers doing the same job
within these two companies would earn different annual incomes.
The possibility of this sort of pay variation historically had been
removed by the union's vigorous efforts.

Although profit sharing introduces the possibility of interfirm variation in earnings, it does so in a manner that at least preserves elements of pattern following. For with profit sharing it is not the case
that there are major differences in the contract terms regulating pay
across Ford and GM. Both companies have similar profit-sharing
plans and, of course, the same other pay provisions concerning the
COLA and AIF formulas. The profit-sharing plans produce differences in pay primarily as a product of differences in company financial
performance. As a result the UAW leadership, with some
justification, can still claim that the tradition of interfirm pattern
following has been preserved with regard to contractual language.

Later Chrysler Negotiations
Subsequent events at Chrysler led to a reinstatement of the traditional
wage rules there. The success of the K model and cost-cutting measures led to an improvement in Chrysler's financial situation and
outlook in the fall of 1982.[18] The negotiation of a new contract at
Chrysler in the fall of 1982 included demands by Chrysler workers
that they receive some of the advantage of this improvement and

compensation for their earlier concessions. At the same time Canadian Chrysler workers were complaining that they were particularly hard hit by the COLA freeze included in the earlier concessions in the face of the rapid pace of inflation in Canada.

After rank-and-file rejection of an earlier tentative agreement and a strike by Canadian workers, the UAW and Chrysler signed a new one-year agreement in December 1982. The agreement provided an upfront wage increase equivalent to the traditional 3 percent AIF formula increase, fully restored the traditional COLA, and eliminated the profit-sharing plan introduced in 1980. These wage increases amounted to restoration of the historic wage rule, the AIF and COLA increases.[19]

The inclusion of a cost-of-living escalator in a one-year contract might seem a bit unusual; the use of this type of escalator is normally associated with multiyear labor agreements. Yet this agreement can be understood as a compromise between the Chrysler workers' desire to return to the old wage rules and the pressures of Chrysler's uncertain future (hence only a one-year term in the agreement). Revealing some of the limits to his participation on the Chrysler board of directors, during the negotiation of the contract Douglas Fraser temporarily removed himself from the board on grounds that participation during the negotiations would pose a conflict of interest.

Chrysler's financial condition continued to improve over 1983, and the company in the fall of 1983 announced that it would repay its federal loans ahead of schedule. Negotiations were then opened early for the labor contract set to expire on January 14, 1984. In September 1983 Chrysler and the UAW announced the negotiation of a new contract that is scheduled to run until September 1985, one year after the GM and Ford 1982–1984 contracts are scheduled for renegotiation. This agreement includes annual wage increase equivalent to the traditional AIF formula and continues the full COLA escalator.[20] It does not contain any form of profit sharing.

By including the traditional formula increases, this agreement provides further testament to the strong attachment autoworkers have to
traditional wage rules. Its adoption also conveys a belief on the part
of labor and management at Chrysler that the company's economic
troubles are over, which enables the return of the traditional wage
rules.

Heightened worker militance at the shop floor level in Chrysler was
revealed in a local strike in the fall of 1983. A six-day strike at the
Twinsburg stamping plant led to the shutdown of all Chrysler assembly plants, a temporary shortage of certain car models, and reduced
profits in the fourth quarter of 1983 (Bureau of National Affairs, 1983).
The emergence of this shop floor militance along with the signing of a
traditional wage agreement led some observers to claim that traditional bargaining had returned to the auto industry. Many of these
same observers went on to predict that this sort of traditional bargaining would govern during the GM and Ford contract renewals in
September 1984.

Implications of the Changes Made to the Wage Rules
In terms of responding to the new economic conditions faced by the
auto industry, the biggest effect of the modifications made to the
wage and fringe benefit rules comes through their slowing of the rise
in hourly labor costs. The profit-sharing plans at Ford and GM add
flexibility to the industry's compensation package by making wages
somewhat responsive to the companies' financial performance, but
given the relatively small share of autoworkers' compensation determined through profit sharing, this effect is rather small. Consequently the pay concessions provide little assistance to the industry's
efforts to respond to the new economic environment by gaining
greater automatic sensitivity in contract terms to economic
conditions.

The process of wage adjustment was deliberate and revealed the
autoworkers' reluctance to modify the wage rules more significantly

even though enormous layoffs were occurring. The figures presented in chapter 2 (table 2.1) show that from 1950 until the late 1960s, a steady ratio was maintained between autoworkers' hourly earnings and the mean earnings of all production workers in the private sector in the United States. Consequently although the use of wage rules in this period may have brought stability to the negotiations process, it is not so clear how the use of the wage rules affected wage outcomes. One could argue that in the absence of the rules, autoworkers' earnings would have likely followed mean private sector earnings in any case.

Yet the autoworkers' resistance to modify wages more significantly in the face of the massive post-1979 layoffs provides a clear example where the industry's wage rules affected wage outcomes. Furthermore the fact that the wage reductions introduced in the Big Three agreements after 1979 preserved the structure of the wage rules provides additional evidence of autoworkers' persistent strong attachment to the wage rules and provides an illustration of how the presence of wage rules affected the bargaining process.

More generally the auto industry illustrates how wage-setting procedures adopted and used in one economic environment are not easily modified in the face of changes in the economic environment. The COLA and AIF wage rules were introduced and then extended in the auto industry over thirty years in an economic environment of long-run growth in employment and auto sales. The long use of the wage rules made it difficult for autoworkers to accept the fact that after 1979, the economic environment might no longer countenance the continuation of the traditional rules.

Connective Bargaining

The introduction of profit-sharing plans that tie autoworkers' pay levels at least partially to company performance allows for the emergence of variation in employment terms across the auto companies.

This provided an end to strict pattern following at the national contract level, which is important because it weakens a central feature of
the connective bargaining structure within the industry. Yet even
more significant erosion of the connective bargaining structure
occurred as a consequence of events at the plant level.

In the face of plant closings and the high number and prolonged
nature of layoffs, workers and local unions after 1979 started agreeing
to major modifications in their local agreements and local work rule
practices.[21] These changes introduced a significant degree of variation
across plants in contract terms and work practices and in this way
eroded the connective bargaining structure that historically had
prevailed in the industry.

Motivations for Work Rule Changes
At the core the modifications introduced into local practices and contract terms arose out of an effort to avoid further job loss and improve
workers' job security by lowering production costs. Some of the work
rule changes involve direct efforts to lower costs by increasing the
amount of labor effort per dollar of compensation. An example of this
sort of work rule change that was being made in a number of plants
was the tightening of production standards, such as requiring workers on an engine assembly line to work on a greater number of en-
gines per hour than they had in the past. Other work rule changes
involved an effort to lower production costs by increasing the flexibility by which labor was deployed. Common examples of the latter
include reductions (consolidations) in the number of classifications in
a plant or limits imposed on the frequency with which workers could
use their seniority rights to transfer to a different job.

Although all of these work rule changes in broad terms entailed reductions in production costs, a number of more specific motivations
arose for the changes. It is worth tracing those various motivations
because each implied something different for the local and national
union.

In part local work rule modification arose as an extension of the national efforts to lower production costs as a way to increase job security. In the negotiations at Chrysler, Ford, and GM, significant pay concessions were agreed to by the UAW after 1979. Since production costs are also strongly affected by work practices that are often set in the local agreements, the modification of local agreements complemented efforts to lower costs by revising the national contract.

Across plants that were engaged in similar production processes in the same company, perfect standardization had never been attained in local work practices. Some of the variation in work practices resulted from small differences in local contract language. In some other cases there were informal agreements between labor and management that had lowered production standards or in other ways changed work practices so as to raise the plant's production costs above those in other plants in the company producing the same part or operation. Once labor and management began to modify work practices as part of efforts to respond to the economic slump, their focus often turned to removing inequities that had emerged across plants over the years. Workers who had been able to establish particularly favorable working conditions found themselves under intense pressure to bring those work practices closer to the operating standards within other plants. In contrast to the other work rule changes being adopted, these changes brought greater standardization in work practices across plants.

Threat of Outsourcing
A different motivation for local work rule modification existed in plants where management had the opportunity to outsource by purchasing the part or service from a company not covered by the terms of the UAW's national auto agreements. Within all of the Big Three companies there are some plants engaged in parts production, as well as plants that assemble these parts or put together the final car (the assembly plants). These parts plants are covered by the terms of each

company's national agreement with the UAW and a supplementary local agreement. The important distinction between the various types of plants is that parts plants face the greatest pressure from the threat of outsourcing. Potential alternative suppliers of the parts include plants outside the Big Three unionized by the UAW or some other union, nonunion domestic companies, and foreign parts producers.

The decline in auto sales has led management to look increasingly to such outsourcing as a way to lower costs (Altshuler et al. 1984). Factors providing an incentive for this include the relative rise in autoworkers' compensation as compared to other workers in and outside the United States (table 3.1). In addition the fact that technological advances made in the auto industry have spread to other firms outside the industry contributes to the number of competing suppliers. Furthermore foreign local content and import requirements have led auto management to increase foreign sourcing in order to maintain access to some foreign markets. But as with so many other things, the most significant pressure for greater outsourcing was the low level of sales and the heightened level of foreign competition that led auto management to search more aggressively for ways to lower production costs. Although lower-cost parts suppliers may have existed in the past, the industry's economic success limited the pressure for their use.

Workers facing the threat that management would turn to outsourcing as a substitute for in-house production responded in many plants by supporting major changes in local work practices. An axle plant in one of the Big Three companies provides an example of this process.

Work Rule Changes Adopted in One Plant
Employment in this plant in late 1982 stood at 2,700 hourly workers as compared to 1978 employment of 8,000. The plant's management stated to the local union in the fall of 1981 that unless significant work rule concessions were provided, a new axle for front-wheel-drive cars and the axles for some new truck models would be purchased from

foreign suppliers, and the plant likely would be closed within a few years. The local union debated the proposed changes and then voted to accept a revised local agreement formalizing many of the work rule changes. Under the new agreement, throughout the plant: production standards are raised; job bidding rights are modified to reduce the frequency of intraplant transfers; and production classifications are broadened so as to include some incidental machine maintenance, inspection, and housekeeping tasks previously performed either by craft workers or other production workers. In addition in the work areas producing parts for the new models (some areas of the plant will continue to produce rear-drive axles for old models), a number of other work rule changes were adopted: the creation of a single classification for all production workers, further limitations on job bidding and transfer rights, and the consideration of ability along with seniority in promotions in contrast to a former strict seniority criterion.

This plant is an interesting case because it also illustrates that workers are often willing to grant these work rule concessions only if an explicit increase in employment follows. The local agreement that provided the work rule concessions stipulated that the changes were being adopted so as to bring new business into the plant. In the spring of 1983 corporate management changed their plans and, before starting production of a new axle for front-wheel-drive cars in this plant shifted production of the car axle to another site. After a series of heated discussions, management agreed to rescind many of the work rule changes adopted in the plant although the single production classification system and other work rule changes continued in the work areas of the plant where axles were being built for new front-wheel-drive trucks.

The same need for an explicit linkage between work rule changes and enhanced employment security is revealed in other work rule changes being negotiated in this plant. One example is provided by craft workers in the plant who were willing to increase production standards and experiment with intercraft flexibility (for example, by allowing electricians to perform some minor welding) when these changes led to the explicit introduction of new business into the plant (the repair of programmable control panels). Another example was provided when craft workers responsible for repairing hydraulic machinery agreed to greater intercraft flexibility when management agreed not to subcontract the repair job out of the plant.

The same experience occurred in many of the plants I visited. In order to bring in-house the repair work associated with new programmable machinery, craft workers in a number of plants were willing to increase production standards (reduce the time it takes to perform the proposed job) and experiment with team forms of work that broadened the responsibilities of craft workers. Other craft workers in these plants who did not see an explicit employment gain from similar work rule changes frequently opposed these changes.[22]

One could argue that there always exists an implicit trade-off between work rules and employment levels.[23] This results from the fact that modifications in work rules can lead to lower costs, which in turn lead to reductions in the price of autos, an expansion in auto sales, and eventually an expansion in auto employment. Yet it appears that workers do not always see these connections. Instead management's initiatives on the shop floor often center around efforts to convince workers and their unions that such a correspondence in fact does exist.

Problems for the National Union
The process of local work rule modification creates a number of problems for the national union. The existence of significant diversity across plants in work practices often leads to rivalries and jealousies. Workers in two different plants that might be only a few blocks or miles apart will readily learn about differences in work practices and exert pressure within their local or on the national union to ensure that their own work conditions match the best around.

Once diversity is allowed into the system, the national union repeatedly faces questions regarding when to allow a plant to modify its work practices in a manner different from the norm. The possibility always looms that management will use local work rule changes to whipsaw the union by repeatedly going to plants and demanding that they adopt a work rule concession first won in another plant.[24] The viability of that strategy comes from management's threat to shift production to plants that more extensively revise their local agreements. Consequently the threat of such whipsawing is greater where there exists more than one plant within a company producing the same product.

The national union's task is to monitor the process so as to allow local plants to make work rule changes that are truly necessary to compete against external suppliers and to allow those work rule changes deemed to supplement national cost reduction efforts but to prevent local unions from getting into a vicious cycle of interplant competition. Distinguishing between these different kinds of work rule changes is not an easy task. In part it was the desire to avoid such distinctions that prompted the national union to favor strict pattern following across plants in the traditional connective bargaining structure.

Work Rule Changes as an Amendment to Connective Bargaining
The process by which local work rule changes occurred illustrates how strongly the parties resisted major modifications to the traditional labor relations system. Interviews conducted with local management and union officials reveal that a number of local unions began to modify significantly their local agreements in mid-1981. Sometimes the national union offices of the UAW were not fully informed of these changes. In some other cases the national union was informed and did provide an informal sanction for the agreed-on changes. However, it was only in the national contracts signed at Ford and GM in the spring of 1982 that the union adopted an official policy regarding local work rule contract changes, and even then the

official policy did not conform to actual practice. In the 1982 Ford and GM contracts the national union formally empowered local unions to modify local work rule practices when faced by a major outsourcing decision with the following contract language:

In the event that changes in labor costs can make a difference in the reasons for outsourcing action, the Union shall have 30 days from the notice to propose any changes in work practices or any local deviation from the Collective Bargaining Agreement that might make it feasible for the company to continue to produce without being economically disadvantaged. (Ford Motor Company 1982b, p. 39)

This new clause legitimized a wide range of work rule concessions but in a manner that illustrates the national union's desire to preserve as much as possible of the old bargaining structure. For instance, the new clause appeared in a memorandum of understanding concerning outsourcing that supplements the national contract and not in the main part of the contract where national versus local union respon-sibilities are delineated. Furthermore the narrow range of the clause did not hold in practice. Field interviews reveal that local unions continued to engage in work rule modifications long after the 1982 contracts were signed even where outsourcing was not an issue. These local unions were responding to one of the other pressures: either changing work rules in the aftermath of enormous declines in plant employment or modifying local practices so as to bring the plant's work practices into alignment with the practices in other plants in the company producing the same part or operation.

Implications for the Bargaining System
Since the opportunity for outsourcing varied enormously across plants, one of the important products of increased outsourcing is that it led to varying work rule concessions across plants. Increased local variation in work rules also arose as a natural consequence of the decentralized nature of the work rule changes. The net effect of this interplant divergence in work practices was to reduce the standard-ization that was part of the traditional connective bargaining struc-ture; however, it is important to note that when the parties modified

their well-connected labor relations system, they did so in a manner maintaining the appearance of the system's full preservation. Furthermore, as with workers' attachment to wage rules, the long history of connective bargaining made workers and the UAW reluctant to abandon this key feature of the traditional bargaining system, and they did so only under the pressure of large actual or threatened employment declines.

Often the modification of local work rules and contracts involved a complicated interaction with ongoing worker participation programs. In this way the erosion of the connective bargaining structure in the auto labor relations system was linked to changes in another part of that system: shifts away from the traditional job control focus in bargaining. The next chapter traces how increases in the amount of worker and union participation in business decision making after 1979 led to a movement away from the traditional job control focus and to further movement away from connective bargaining. Tracing the history of worker participation programs is important because these programs played a critical role in the labor relations changes adopted between 1979 and 1983. But understanding these worker participation programs is also important because the future expansion of these programs may play a significant role in the industry's long-run strategic response to the changing world auto industry.

4   The Evolution of QWL Programs and Other Shifts away from a Job Control Focus

The relationship between labor and management in the auto industry traditionally has been centered around job control unionism. Notable features of this type of unionism include the formal, arms-length nature of collective bargaining and the heavy reliance on written procedures. In addition much of the contractual regulation of workplace rules centers around a job classification system and the linking of wages, rights, and the duties of workers to detailed job classifications.

A number of the changes introduced into auto labor relations after 1979 move the parties away from this job control orientation. These changes include steps taken at the national level, such as the inclusion of Douglas Fraser, then UAW president, on the board of directors of the Chrysler Corporation in 1979 and a more informal exchange of information between national union leaders and top corporate management in the Big Three companies. Other steps were taken at the plant level, including quality circles, the creation of mutual growth forums, and informal communication channels between labor and management.

Although changes introduced at the national level (in particular the placement of Fraser on the Chrysler board) received a lot of press coverage, developments underway in shop floor practices are more significant for these changes strike at the heart of the traditional job control system.

Early QWL Programs

The auto industry's experimentation with worker participation programs began in the early 1970s. The rise in shop floor work militance
and the well-publicized strike at the GM Lordstown plant in 1972
triggered wide-ranging discussions in and out of the auto industry
concerning the workplace environment, worker motivation, and potential avenues that might be used to enrich work and solve U.S.
industry's absentee and productivity problems. (For example, see
Work in America 1973.) In addition the diversity in the tenor of labor-
management relations that perennially existed across auto plants suggested the potential benefits of programs focused around improving
worker attitudes.

The first QWL programs launched in the auto industry included experiments replacing the assembly line with work teams and programs
focused on improving the communication between workers and their
supervisors.[1] The models for many of the early QWL programs in the
United States were the well-publicized programs underway in the
Swedish auto industry.[2]

In 1973 a letter of understanding was added to the national UAW-GM
agreement (and a similar letter was included in agreements with Ford
and Chrysler) stating:

In discussions prior to the opening of the current negotiations for a
new collective bargaining agreement, General Motors Corporation
and the UAW gave recognition to the desirability of mutual effort to
improve the quality of work life for the employees. In consultation
with Union representatives, certain projects have been undertaken by
management in the field of organizational development, involving
the participation of represented employees. These and other projects
and experiments improve the quality of work life, thereby advantaging the worker by making work a more satisfying experience, advantaging the Corporation by leading to a reduction in employee
absenteeism and turnover, and advantaging the consumer through
improvement in the quality of the products manufactured. (General
Motors Corporation 1982, pp. 275–276)

At GM a joint national committee including representatives from labor and management was created to encourage and review the variety of experimental projects that followed. Among these projects was a program to improve communication between workers and managers accompanied by a survey of worker attitudes, which showed signs of early success at the GM-Lakewood assembly plant (Dowling 1975). At a van assembly plant in Detroit, assembly line operations in one work station were replaced by a team (stall) work organization where workers performed a long cycle of job tasks in contrast to the traditional short cycle of assembly tasks (Harvard Business School 1976). Focused on improving worker-supervisor relations, the QWL program at the GM-Tarrytown plant was heralded as successfully reducing absentee and grievance rates and improving worker attitudes in the mid-1970s (Guest 1979).

The pace and extent of these experimental programs varied widely within companies and across the industry. At Ford the development of such programs stalled after a few unsuccessful pilot projects and a lack of enthusiasm on the part of the national steering committee.[3] Few participation projects were initiated at Chrysler or American Motors.

At GM, where the widest diversity of programs emerged under the enthusiastic leadership of Irving Bluestone, then vice-president of the UAW and director of its GM Department, there were some early failures as well as successes. The new cooperative relationship at the Lakewood assembly plant lasted only a few years, evaporating when plant management changed and large layoffs occurred in 1975. The team van assembly project failed to reach performance expectations and soon ended. Other pilot projects that tried to replace the traditional assembly line with team-style production also were short-lived. On the whole the use of team-style production as a replacement for the assembly line mode of production was not a common feature of the participation programs in the U.S. auto industry.[4]

For the union the potential advantage of the QWL programs was that they might be useful as a vehicle to provide workers with improvements in conditions on the shop floor, such as better lighting and improved ventilation, and in other ways provide a more comfortable work environment. Since the end of World War II, the UAW had negotiated a number of major additions to its fringe benefit package, including better pensions, health insurance, additional holidays and vacations, and supplementary insurance benefits. The QWL programs initiated in the early 1970s can be understood from the union's perspective as essentially one more addition to the benefit package. Having already won so many hard fringe benefits and confronting militance on the shop floor regarding workplace conditions, the union was turning its attention toward softer workplace issues by means of the early QWL programs.

At the plant level this supplemental nature of the early QWL programs was preserved through the maintenance of a clear and sharp separation between QWL activities and normal collective bargaining issues and procedures. This kind of separation is symbolized by a statement made in 1980 by Irving Bluestone that a guiding principle of QWL programs is "the provisions of the national agreement and of the local agreements and practices remain inviolable" (Bluestone 1980, p. 40). Bluestone went on to state that where QWL is introduced, "The local understands that normal collective bargaining continues" (ibid., p. 40).[5]

Management's efforts to maintain a separation of QWL activities and normal collective bargaining was indicated by the fact that the plant-level management staffs delegated to support the QWL programs typically were under the control of the plant personnel staff (whose normal primary area of concern was salaried employees) rather than the plant industrial relations staff. This structure was mirrored at the corporate level. At General Motors, from 1973 until a reorganization in 1981, the corporate QWL staff was part of the personnel department rather than the labor relations department.

Thus the early QWL programs in the U.S. auto industry were con-
ceived and viewed as an experimental supplement to collective bargaining. Labor and management did not perceive that a fundamental
reorganization of collective bargaining was required. Rather QWL
activities were viewed as additions to the existing collective bargaining system. This is not to say that some supporters did not see a
greater potential for QWL programs; nonetheless these programs remained a supplement to and not a fundamental alteration in shop
floor labor relations; they were programs primarily oriented toward
improving the workplace environment and workers' relationships
with their supervisors.

In some GM plants throughout the mid- and late 1970s, there were
continuing successes in the early QWL programs, but overall the
growth and impact of the programs was fairly limited until the industry's slump after 1979 triggered a new wave of cooperative programs.
Chapter 5 analyzes data drawn from two divisions within GM and
traces the growth of the QWL programs in those plants until 1980.
The quantitative data reveal the limited growth of these early QWL
programs. For instance, in one division as of 1979, only 9.5 percent of
the hourly work force was involved in any QWL program. Statistical
analysis of these data also reveals that these early QWL programs had
a limited impact on plant-level industrial relations and economic
performance.

QWL Programs after 1979

At both GM and Ford the industry's economic slump after 1979 induced management to search more aggressively for ways to cut costs.
An expansion of worker participation programs grew out of this cost-
cutting effort in a number of ways. In the face of the attention drawn
to Japan's economic success and industrial practices, management
came to appreciate more fully that workers possess valuable knowledge about the production process. This knowledge might include
awareness of machine idiosyncrasies or ideas about how to coordi-

nate the flow of materials through the plant. The task was then to create a mechanism that would recognize these ideas better. QWL programs came to be seen as a vehicle that might help bring to the surface workers' ideas about improvements in the production process.

A second justification for the increased emphasis on QWL programs was the belief that worker participation might also lower costs through the creation of more cooperative relations between workers and their supervisors. The idea here was not to focus on the role that better attitudes would play directly in cost reduction but rather to take advantage of the fact that better relations would help smooth the administration of the collective bargaining agreement. The daily administration of national and local agreements involves a number of issues that sometimes become the source of heated disagreements between labor and management. A critical influence on plant-level performance is the extent to which labor and management are able to resolve disagreements and avoid any attendant disruption. It was believed that QWL programs might help to improve these labor-management shop floor relations.

Worker participation programs also became attractive because labor often was willing to make modifications to work rules that brought either direct cost savings or improved flexibility in human resource allocation if those changes were accompanied by an increase in worker participation in decision making.

The economic pressure to expand cooperative programs was supported by some changes simultaneously occurring in corporate and union personnel. At Ford the growth of cooperative programs was spurred in 1980 by the appointment of Don Ephlin as vice-president of the UAW and director of its Ford Department and Pete Pestillo as the Ford vice-president of industrial relations, both of whom strongly supported cooperative endeavors. At GM an increase in higher management's commitment to QWL was signaled by the appointment of

Alfred Warren, Jr., as the corporate vice-president of labor relations to fill a spot left vacant by the retirement of George Morris, who had generally opposed cooperative programs. Warren had formerly headed the group in the corporate personnel department in charge of QWL programs.[6]

With their focus on cost containment, the participation programs acquired an emphasis different from both programs underway in the United States in the early 1970s and programs operating within Swedish industry. As the scope of QWL programs expanded, the programs began to include major changes in work rules and interact closely with traditional collective bargaining processes.

Where QWL-type programs took hold, the central task that emerged for the union was to mediate the interaction between cooperative programs and collective bargaining processes. This was to cause some problems for the UAW by creating a need for the union to identify its own vision of the cooperative programs. This problem is illustrated by the plant described next.

A Piecemeal Participation Program

Participation programs began in this plant in 1980 in the aftermath of enormous layoffs and the emergence of the possibility that the plant would be closed if conditions continued to deteriorate over the next couple of years. This plant manufactures parts for the Ford Motor Company. Employment in the plant had peaked in 1979 at 3,400 hourly workers and by 1982 had fallen to 1,400. Labor relations in the plant had been, in the words of the local union's bargaining chairman, "extremely adversarial."

Facing layoffs and frustrated by their previous acrimonious relationship, however, labor and management set out in early 1980 to experiment with a worker participation process. The local union shortly discovered that language encouraging such programs, had been included in the company's 1979 national agreement. Following the guidelines of the national agreement and with the advice and encouragement provided by national UAW officers, labor and management in this plant embarked on a series of cooperative programs.

The participation program initially centered around the creation of employee involvement (EI) groups, which operated essentially as quality circles; on a voluntary basis workers would meet for one hour a week (on paid time) and discuss workplace issues. By the summer of 1983 these groups included 20 percent of the plant's hourly work force. Expansion of the EI groups was limited by two factors: the disruptive influence of continuing layoffs and the large resources needed for group start-up. Specific issues that have been addressed by the EI groups in this plant include the placement of a conveyor belt, the improvement of gauging operations, better lighting, and the rearrangement of some work stations to coordinate work operations better.

The local union has made sure that contractual problems are not discussed in the EI groups. If issues such as job jurisdiction or production standards come up, the discussion is halted by the union committeeman who stays abreast of the activities within the EI groups in the area of the plant in his jurisdiction. For instance, some EI groups began to discuss whether workers within the group should take over some of the inspection job tasks previously performed by separate inspectors as a way to improve quality control. This was deemed to be a contractual issue and was sent to the union's bargaining committee, where it was discussed in negotiations with management.

The limits imposed on discussions within the EI groups, however, have not prevented the emergence of a substantial interaction between cooperative programs and traditional collective bargaining procedures and issues. In some departments in this plant, the EI groups have led to this interaction. A few groups have contacted parts vendors to help resolve production problems. One group performed a feasibility study for a robot and in the process influenced the purchase decision of the plant's engineering staff. Where changes in the product mix or the introduction of new machinery lead to a major change in the layout of a work area, the workers in the area are now typically consulted beforehand. Plant industrial engineers meet with the workers to review the proposed changes and solicit their recommendations regarding the layout changes.

On a track separate from the EI groups, the relationship between union officers and plant management was changing. Union officers were being provided with information regarding business plans and upcoming events in the plant, a process that contrasted sharply with past behavior. For the first time the plant manager was forewarning union officials about upcoming layoffs and new machinery and asking for their advice regarding how these changes might best be implemented. Some of these discussions have occurred as part of mutual growth forums, which follow the guidelines outlined in the 1982 national Ford-UAW contract. More often these discussions occurred on an informal basis.

A significant amount of the communication between plant and union officials concerned the competitive pressures faced by the plant and steps that might be taken to lower in-house production costs so as to compete more successfully for new business. As a parts supplier this plant confronted the fact that Ford corporate management was deciding whether to purchase the parts produced by this plant from suppliers outside Ford or have them produced in other plants within Ford. Discussions regarding these competitive pressures led to a new local agreement in 1982 that modified a number of work rules in the plant. This local agreement supplemented the new national Ford-UAW contract, which had been negotiated in the spring of 1982.

The new local contract included agreements to increase production standards; have production workers perform some housekeeping, inspection, and incidental maintenance job functions; alter overtime and shift preference arrangements; and allow production workers to assist skilled tradesmen in the repair of machines. These concessions were provided by the local union on the condition that they would lead to the arrival of new business in the plant (the plant would become a parts supplier for some of Ford's new models). It was also agreed that workers would be selected into the work areas involved in any new business with some consideration of ability rather than rely exclusively on existing contractual seniority provisions. (These work rule changes are similar to the changes introduced in the plant described in chapter 3.)

In one work area in the plant where new business was brought in, a single (universal) classification system has been adopted. Formerly there were ten separate job classifications covering production workers in this department; there is now only one classification. The original plan was to include a pay-for-knowledge system where workers would receive higher pay on mastering a wider variety of job tasks in this work area. At the time of my last visit to the plant, implementation issues regarding the rates of pay tied to the various steps in the proposed new pay system had led to a postponement in the implementations of the new pay system.

Management in this plant hopes that the positive experience with the single classification system will encourage the system's expansion to other work areas in the plant. The use of a single classification in one work area and management's hopes for expansion of its use highlights the fact that in many ways the events in this plant represent an effort to move gradually to the operating team approach adopted within a few GM plants where all production workers in a plant are in a single job classification.

One illustration of this movement is that discussion in the Ford parts plant recently has focused around shifting the EI groups to a department team basis. Like the use of a single classification system, this shift entails a fundamental redirection of the participation process. At the core the issue is how the participation process can be linked more closely with work rule issues and thereby to many of the issues currently resolved through collective bargaining processes. From management's view the need to integrate worker participation processes and work rule issues more closely arises from their concern that the participation process not only address housekeeping issues but also focus on the problems affecting the plant's economic viability and competitive position with alternative suppliers.

To date work rule issues and the EI process largely have been kept procedurally apart. This has created two central problems. First, by not focusing on work rules, the agenda within the EI groups has been limited to the point that some employees have become disillusioned with the outputs of the process. Furthermore insecurities have arisen within the work force regarding job and seniority rights. Employees are hesitant to give up the traditional classification system and experiment with a single classification system because the job specifications and seniority rights embedded in the traditional system provide protection from supervisory abuse. Workers fear that managers will abuse the discretion available in a more open single classification system during matters such as the distribution of work assignments or disciplinary actions. If the security and protection now provided through the detailed classification and rule system are given up, the workers want something to be put in its place.

Although union officials have acquired more participation and information regarding business decisions in this plant, this has occurred in a manner largely disassociated from other programs in the plant and, perhaps most important, has not fully involved the hourly work force. Thus although significant change has occurred in labor-management relations, a series of problems exist that jeopardize the future of the worker participation process. First, both workers and managers complain that many of the EI groups are in need of reinvigoration. Second, the pace by which work rule changes have been adopted and classification systems revised has slowed due to resistance from some work groups. Third, debilitating problems, such as whether participation in the new department teams or in a new statistical quality control program is voluntary (as with the EI groups), have slowed the adoption of these programs. Additionally there is a sense of unease within both union and management concerning where the participation process is headed and how the process relates to the economic pressures facing the plant.

It is difficult to imagine how a piecemeal expansion of the cooperative programs in this plant could occur. The problem with the current mode of operation is that it requires the local union to mediate continually the tensions between the so-called cooperative programs and the work rule changes made through traditional collective bargaining channels. The local union is continually pressed to answer the claims of some workers in the plant that the participation process is being abused and should be ended because it is leading to work rule changes, an issue some argue it never was supposed to address. Thereby the local union is forced into a defensive position regarding work rule changes because it has no consistent way to argue that the participation programs and the work rule changes are all part of the same basic set of issues.

This is not to say that the local union would have an easy job if some sort of institutional link was provided to the participation process and basic collective bargaining processes. There would still remain legitimate disagreement within labor's ranks regarding how much to modify work rules and where to take the labor-management relationship. Nonetheless it is difficult to see how the parties would have a chance to resolve these issues unless this sort of linkage developed.

It would seem that either the participation program would expand to the point that it entailed a more fundamental reorganization of work and shop floor labor relations, or it would retrench to the point where work rule changes were stopped and the remaining participation program centered around EI groups (or some other quality circle type of activity). In the latter scenario the involvement groups would have the limited goal of addressing housekeeping issues and providing a forum for hourly workers and supervisors to discuss problems informally.

Diversity of Experiences and Union Leader Views

All plants did not develop extensive QWL-type programs after 1979. In some plants virtually no cooperative programs developed, and shop floor labor relations continue in a manner similar to the traditional pattern. This happened in some cases because influential managers, local union leaders, or workers opposed either the concept of labor-management cooperation or the changes associated with the cooperative programs.[7] In some other plants, cooperative programs were tried but eventually disappeared.

The diversity in local union leaders' views toward QWL programs is revealed in a survey and interviews I conducted with Thomas Kochan and Nancy Mower (Kochan, Katz, and Mower 1984). Our research surveyed 110 local union officers, including local presidents, executive board members, and shop committeemen, in five plants of one of the major auto companies in the fall of 1982. The survey asked questions regarding the union leaders' views toward the cooperative programs underway in their plants. All of these plants had some sort of QWL-type program underway for at least six months, although the intensity of the programs varied widely across the plants. Both corporate management and union leaders in this company believed that the programs underway in these five plants were somewhat more extensive than the average QWL-type program in the company. This suggests that union leaders' attitudes toward participation programs in these plants are probably more favorable than the attitudes of local union leaders in the average plant.

The survey results that follow show that in general the local union leaders were supportive of the QWL programs and felt that workers and the union would benefit in the long run from the programs.[8] For example, in question 3, 81.7 percent of the surveyed union leaders encouraged workers to participate in the cooperative programs. In question 5, 58.0 percent of the surveyed union leaders responded that they thought the cooperative programs would either probably or definitely strengthen the local union. A favorable attitude toward the cooperative programs also showed up in the interviews I conducted with union leaders in these plants.

At the same time, the figures, particularly the responses to question 4, reveal that there is a significant minority of local union leaders who feel that the cooperative programs are undermining the grievance and other collective bargaining procedures. For example, in question 4 e, 19.3 percent of the union leaders agreed or strongly agreed with the view that the participation programs would undermine the union's ability to enforce the contract. In question 4 a, 21.0 percent of the union leaders agreed or strongly agreed with the view that the participation programs interfered with the proper role of the grievance procedure.

Question 1: *What do you think the union's role ought to be in the QWL process? (check one)*

The union should oppose the program. 3.7
The union should remain neutral but not actively participate in the process. 12.0
The union should support and actively participate in running the program with management. 84.3

Question 2: *If we were to come back five years from now, what kind of QWL process do you think we would find here?*

The QWL process will have ended by then. 13.8
The QWL process will look about the same as it is today. 21.1
The QWL process will have grown and expanded. 65.1

Question 3: *If workers ask you about whether they should participate in the QWL program, what do you generally advise? (check one)*

I encourage them to participate. 81.7
I don't take a position one way or the other. 17.4
I discourage them from participating. .9

Question 4: *Below are listed a number of things that some people believe a QWL process might do to the job of a union representative or shop committee member. We would like your opinion. To what extent do you agree that the QWL process has:*

	Strongly Disagree	Disagree	Neither Agree nor Disagree	Agree	Strongly Agree
a. Interfered with the proper role of the grievance procedure.	23.8	29.5	25.7	18.1	2.9
b. Given workers another channel to get their problems solved.	2.8	5.5	6.4	64.2	21.1
c. Reduced member interest in the union.	17.9	29.2	34.0	13.2	5.7
d. Improved the ability of union representatives to solve problems or complaints workers bring to them.	3.7	14.8	23.1	43.5	14.8
e. Undermined the union's ability to enforce the contract.	28.4	33.9	18.3	13.8	5.5
f. Improved the union's communications with its members.	2.8	15.0	30.8	36.4	15.0

Question 5: *Overall, what effect do you think the QWL process will have on the union in your plant?*

Definitely Weaken	Probably Weaken	No Effect	Probably Strengthen	Definitely Strengthen
8.4	12.1	21.5	34.6	23.4

Note: One hundred ten local union leaders in five auto plants responded to this survey. For more details of the survey, see Kochan, Katz, and Mower 1984.

The survey results and interviews conducted in the five plants are consistent with what I heard in the plant described in detail earlier and in other plants. The central problem for the union that emerged as cooperative programs developed after 1979 is to mediate the interaction between worker participation programs and traditional collective bargaining procedures and processes. This problem developed in large part because as the participation programs began to address work rule issues, the separation previously maintained between participation programs and collective bargaining was no longer viable. An even closer link was forged between worker participation and basic collective bargaining issues and processes in GM's plants that adopted an operating team system.

Operating Team System

By the end of 1983 ten GM plants organized work and labor relations around an operating team system. The operating team system entails a single production worker job classification and other shop floor labor relations practices that are far different from the traditional job control focus.

As a fundamental alternative to traditional labor relations practices, the team system is worthy of careful analysis. Furthermore, as exemplified by the plant just described, it appears that where QWL-type programs have taken hold, labor and management quickly confront the problem of mediating the relationship between cooperative programs and traditional collective bargaining procedures. The team system seems to provide a successful way of merging worker participation and work rule changes. The team system also is worthy of analysis because where labor and management have modified work rules extensively in an effort to reduce costs, they have moved in the direction of a team style of work organization. The use of the team system is growing through the complete adoption of the system in a number of new GM plants. Among the facilities that have recently adopted the team system are GM's new assembly plants in Orion, Pontiac, Wentzville, St. Louis, and downtown Detroit.

History of the Use of Teams
Work organization systems similar to GM's operating team system have been used in nonunion plants since the 1950s.[9] Exact figures on

the usage of team-type work systems are not available; however, it appears that the use of team systems in nonunion plants increased significantly in the United States over the 1960s and 1970s.[10]

GM first introduced the system into a few of its southern plants. Initially workers in these plants did not have union representation, and the plants were often referred to as GM's southern strategy. The fact that the team system was first used in nonunion plants heightened workers' and the union's fears that the team system would inevitably erode worker identification and solidarity with the union. In this way the use of teams in some plants became interconnected with the question of union status. The evolution of events at GM's plants in Albany, Georgia, and Oklahoma City illustrates the different courses taken in this interaction between the use of teams and union status.

The Delco-Remy facility in Albany, Georgia, which opened in 1978, was one of the first of GM's plants to use the operating team system. The plant first opened as an unorganized facility. Then GM agreed to apply the transfer of operation clause in its national contract with the UAW and automatically recognized the UAW.[11] During the negotiation of the plant's first local collective bargaining agreement, workers initially resisted the use of the single classification scheme in the plant, and a strike ensued after an impasse was reached over this and other issues. The strike was settled after Irving Bluestone, then head of the UAW's GM Department, consulted with local union officials regarding management's proposals. The local union eventually accepted the team system after management agreed to some modifications in their original plans although the basic elements of the team system adopted in the Albany plant follow the structure used in other team plants.

Events at GM's Oklahoma City assembly plant took a different course. There the team system was also introduced in a facility that was not under UAW representation. The union then tried to organize the plant, and a series of heated and controversial representation elections were held in the late 1970s. In 1976, as part of a new national contract, GM had pledged to remain neutral in the representation election campaigns occurring in its southern plants.[12] During the union representation election campaign that followed in Oklahoma City, there was a lot of controversy regarding whether GM management was truly maintaining the neutrality it had pledged to follow in the face of an active campaign by some of the plant's employees opposing the union's right to represent the work force. In the process many of the workers sympathetic to the union at Oklahoma City came to feel that the team system had been used as a device to help management keep the plant unorganized.

In the national GM-UAW 1979 agreement GM agreed to an accretion clause whereby in any new facilities whose production was closely related to existing production, the UAW would be automatically recognized as the bargaining agent. GM went even further in 1982 when it agreed to recognize automatically the UAW without a formal representation election if the union could produce cards showing that a majority of the workers in a plant favored the UAW. By 1982 the union had used these rights to organize all of the nonunion facilities.

In Oklahoma City the UAW won election as the representative of the work force in 1979 and proceeded to negotiate its first local contract. The local union negotiated forcefully for the removal of the team system, a stance apparently motivated by workers' lingering feelings that the use of the team system was linked to the company's efforts to operate the plant on a nonunion basis. In the local agreement that emerged, the team system was replaced by a classification system that closely followed the form of traditional local agreements, although the Oklahoma City local contract does contain a smaller number of total classifications (production and skilled) than the typical traditional local UAW agreement.

Events at Oklahoma City illustrate a broader point: that it is extremely difficult for labor and management to shift to a more open participatory form of labor relations where the union is fearful of its basic security and representation rights. Whether GM management was in fact using the team system as a device to operate on a nonunion basis or to weaken workers' loyalty to the UAW was irrelevant. The important fact was that a significant number of workers came to believe so. The team system, like other participatory labor relations systems, contains risks for workers and the union by reducing the security provided through the traditional adherence to the detailed written contract. It is unlikely that many workers or unions would be willing to take the gambles associated with the shift to this sort of system unless basic security interests are clearly protected.

There was no counterpart to the operating team plants in Ford, although in a number of Ford plants a few departments have recently adopted single classification systems. Two factors contributed to GM's ability to experiment with the use of team systems. GM first tried out the operating team design in southern plants and then later introduced the system in a few northern plants. In this way the southern and initially nonunion plants functioned as a testing ground for this labor relations approach. In addition GM introduced the team system in either new or completely refurbished plants. The new southern plants are examples of this, but it was also the case that in the north the operating team system was introduced into new or refurbished plants. GM's Buick 81, Cadillac-Livonia, and the new assembly plants fit this pattern.

The explanation for this diffusion pattern seems to be that workers hired in or transferred to new facilities either tend to be more willing to accept the use of new labor relations concepts or have developed less bargaining power to resist the new programs.[13] Furthermore, since new or refurbished plants tend to be associated with the expansion in the output of particular parts or services, employment prospects in the new or refurbished plants are relatively secure. Thus workers in these plants are less likely to fear that the new work systems will lead to job displacement and may contribute to the workers' willingness to use the team system. Since Ford has faced larger sales downturns than GM in recent years and was not opening facilities, it did not have equivalent new facilities in which to introduce the operating team or similar systems.

Design and Operation of the Operating Team System

In the team system, the traditional job classification system, which in some plants amounts to over one-hundred separate job classifications for production workers, is replaced by one in which all workers are in the same classification. In some plants the team system has been adopted for skilled tradesmen as well as production workers, although in these plants there typically remain on the order of seven to ten distinct trades classifications. In some other plants the trades have maintained the traditional set of classifications while production workers are within a single classification.

The detailed description of the team system presented here applies to the use of teams for production workers although some of the same attributes hold where the system is applied to skilled tradesmen. Material for this description is drawn from interviews I conducted with workers, union leaders, and management staffs from four GM plants that utilize the team system.

The central unit of the team system is a work team following functional department lines containing ten to fifteen workers. Collapsing all production worker classifications into a single classification leads to the demise of separate classifications for inspectors, material handlers, and janitors. Instead these job assignments are assigned to the team. Decisions as to how to allocate and accomplish the basic production and auxiliary tasks in the work area are made by the team members under the guidance of a team leader who is a salaried (and hence nonunion) employee taking over many of the responsibilities previously held by the first line supervisor. These decisions are arrived at in regularly scheduled team meetings.

The team meetings serve a number of functions. One task is to set daily work assignments and allocate the various job tasks in the team's work area. It is conceivable that the team would decide to allocate tasks in a highly specialized manner and essentially recreate the old highly specialized job classification system. Typically, however, work assignments made in the teams involve a variety of tasks and in this way bring about a broadening of jobs with production workers taking on some inspection, materials handling, and housekeeping tasks in addition to basic production duties. Workers are encouraged to learn a variety of job tasks within the team's work area by way of a pay-for-knowledge reward scheme. Workers can advance up six pay levels (each level provides roughly 15 cents per hour in additional compensation) by mastering a wider variety of jobs in the work area.

Another important function of the team meetings is to operate as a form of quality circle. The hope is that through participation in these team meetings, workers will become more willing and able to help solve everyday production problems. As part of its analysis of production problems, the team meetings regularly review the costs and revenues associated with the work area. In one team meeting I observed, the team coordinator reviewed the purchase vouchers accumulated by the work area in the previous week and compared the total operating costs of the area to the revenues generated by product outflow from the area.

The work team also has the freedom to develop job rotation schemes and experiment with job redesign. A variety of job rotation patterns exist in the team plants; some teams rotate tasks once a day, and others rotate more or less frequently. More extensive forms of work redesign have not occurred in these plants for a number of reasons. One is that the basic technology in the plants is of standard assembly line type and is designed to operate with short-cycle jobs. Some early experimentation with five-minute cycle jobs did occur in one of the team plants I visited but was abandoned after workers complained that they did not like the longer-cycle jobs. Consequently the use of work teams has not led to abandonment of assembly line production techniques. Concern for work design occasionally has appeared, however, in the initial design of the team plants such as the inclusion of buffers in the plants' assembly lines.

In addition to involving the production workers more directly in production decision making, the operation of the team system provides workers with information regarding issues that under the traditional labor relations system were deemed to be exclusive managerial functions. For example, as part of their efforts to solve production problems, the work teams often consider the layout of the work area and new technologies. The teams frequently contact parts suppliers and the plant industrial engineering staff in pursuit of these and other issues. Furthermore the teams often see cost and revenue data as part of their consideration of production problems. It is through both the everyday decisions made by the team concerning work allocation and the provision of extensive information to the teams regarding business decisions that the team system leads to expanded worker participation in decision making.

In some team plants the local union, through its representatives on a planning committee, participated in the initial selection of the team coordinators (supervisors) and helped to construct the ongoing supervisor assessment procedures. In these plants the union maintains participation in the selection and movement of supervisors across the work teams. Union committeemen in one of these plants stated that they had the right to veto the appointment of new supervisors to the work teams within their jurisdiction.

By eliminating all of the previously detailed job classifications, the team system removes the attachment of worker rights to job classifications that prevailed in the traditional system. In the traditional job control system, rights regarding such issues as bumpings during layoffs, voluntary transfers across work areas in a plant, and overtime equalization are tied to the classification system through language in the local and national collective bargaining agreements. Some of the procedures traditionally regulated through contract language are passed to the work group in the team system. For instance, in some of the plants utilizing the team concept, the work teams vote on overtime distribution and the distribution of daily work assignments.

Field interviews suggest that in the process by which the team reaches these and other decisions, the supervisor, often called the team coordinator, plays a critical role; it is possible for the supervisor to dominate all of the team decisions. How strongly the decisions reached by the team follow the preferences of the supervisor varies substantially and depends to a significant degree on the relationship each supervisor has with his or her respective work team. And yet in most work teams, workers appear to participate in these decisions through the team meetings. In this way worker participation replaces some of the functions previously served by the job control system.

A number of other decisions previously regulated by the local agreement still are regulated through contract language in the team plants. For instance, the team plants still use plant-level years of seniority to determine layoffs. And typically there are detailed and written regulations regarding the rights of workers to transfer voluntarily from one work team to another.

Yet clearly the net effect of the team system is to reduce the amount of formalization in shop floor rules and transfer some of the regulatory authority previously held by the local contract to the work group. That is one of the basic objectives motivating management to introduce the team system in the first place. The decline in the importance of the written contract in the long run may be the most radical aspect of the team system for shop floor labor relations. For some workers the more immediate problem associated with this transfer is the fact that it reduces the security and protection previously provided by the written agreement.

Potential cost advantages are produced by this system by way of greater coordination among workers who are familiar with a number of tasks; heightened quality control because of the meshing of production and inspection tasks; the ease by which the team can adjust to absenteeism by shifting workers across job tasks; and any improvements that follow from the heightened motivation of workers because of increased variation in their work tasks. In addition to these cost savings, the use of such teams can markedly increase the flexibility and adaptability within the production process. It should be much easier to modify work assignments in response to changes in either demand or technology in a system where workers learn a variety of job tasks.[14]

Impact of the Team System on Workers
The potential benefits of the team system for workers include the involvement they gain in a broader array of business decisions. Furthermore the team meetings provide a forum for discussion concerning such housekeeping issues as lighting, safety, and comfort. To the extent that workers value a broadening of their job tasks, the team system provides this form of job enrichment. At the least the system gives workers the chance to experiment with job rotation and some forms of work redesign. For many workers the pay-for-knowledge scheme also provides the potential to earn higher pay than in their previous jobs. The pay rates for the top levels of the system typically are at or above the rates received by the job-setter classification in the old system, among the highest-paid production jobs. By providing the opportunity for higher pay rates, the pay-for-knowledge system operates as a form of a buyout by trading workers higher pay for their willingness to go along with other features of the team system.[15]

The team system also contains some potential disadvantages for workers, ranging from some minor issues to some of deep and lasting significance. Two minor problems are that some workers under the pay-for-knowledge scheme receive lower rates of pay than they received in the old classification system and the fact that some workers resent that in the team meetings other workers can criticize their participation in the team work effort. These issues, however, do not arise for all workers nor do they raise fundamental issues. One would expect that problems of this sort could be worked out in the long run to the satisfaction of most workers, and, in any case, no change in work organization is likely to lead to the satisfaction of all workers. A more serious problem is that through team decision processes, younger workers often get access to jobs that previously were attained through the exercise of seniority rights. As a result the team system appears to be supported more strongly by younger workers and resisted relatively more by older workers.

More serious problems arose in some team plants as a consequence of the suspicion with which the skilled tradesmen viewed the team and pay-for-knowledge systems. The experiences in one plant are illustrative. In this plant the skilled trades workers initially opposed the team system and therefore are not included in it. A year after the start-up of the team system (which governed only production workers), the skilled workers campaigned to remove the teams and pay-for-knowledge system and forced an election over the issue. (An election occurred because the union initially accepted the team system only on a voluntary basis, and the union's right to withdraw from the system was specified in the plant's local contract.) In the election 65 percent of the total plant work force voted to retain the pay-for-knowledge system; however, management clearly has not been as successful as they had initially hoped in involving skilled tradesmen in the team system in this plant.

The opposition of tradesmen to the team system seems to derive from the fact that trades workers traditionally have relied on strict craft lines to increase their bargaining power and preserve the identity of their craft. Production workers benefit from the team system because it provides more flexibility and versatility in their jobs, along with additional input into decision making. But craft workers always had a lot of versatility and input as a consequence of their craft skills. For them the team system's weakening of their craft identity does not appear to be outweighed by the perceived advantages of any additional input they have into business decisions as part of the operation of the teams.

Impact on the Union
By transferring power to the work group and reducing the importance of the written agreement, the team system fundamentally alters the position of the shop stewards, committeemen, and other local union officials. In the traditional shop floor labor relations system, these individuals are heavily involved in contract application and administration. Their tasks include administering or monitoring the grievance procedure, the job bidding procedure, and the other procedures outlined in detail in the local collective bargaining agreement. Although these written procedures have not been eliminated in the team plants, they have been reduced significantly in scope. Instead of traditional contract administration duties, shop floor union officials in the team plants spend much of their time monitoring the actions taken by the work teams and acting to ensure that these team actions do not violate any clauses that remain in either the local or national collective bargaining agreements.

This raises a number of potential problems for the local unions where the team system is introduced. Some local union officials resent the fact that their jobs change under the new system. Familiar with the old system, they do not want to change their ways. In addition the shift to the team system may reduce their power. In the traditional system local union officials have power because of the discretion they are allowed in the administration of some of the contractual provisions. They also hold power because of the superior knowledge they possess regarding the intricacies of the traditional system. The team system appears to erode these traditional power sources.

In addition some local union officials oppose the team system, charging that it reduces the union's power and erodes worker support for the union. These fears are not unfounded for it is possible that the creation of work teams eventually may lead to a shift in workers' loyalties and identification to the team and away from the union.

Whether the union actually loses power on net once a team system is in place will depend heavily on the extent to which the union's traditional role is replaced by one in which the union becomes involved in a broader set of workplace issues. Experiences at GM suggest that the team system holds open the possibility of this sort of expanded union involvement in two ways. The local unions in some GM team plants are heavily involved in the design and operation of the team system. In these plants a planning committee oversees the design and implementation of the team system and continues to monitor the operation of the teams once they are in place. The local union typically has two representatives on this six-person committee.[16] Another way union involvement could expand in the team system is by way of more informal exchanges of information between union officials and plant management. In some team plants the local union receives extensive information regarding layoff and production plans and financial data on the plant's performance and relative standing within its division.

Problems for the national and local unions also result from the variation is pay and work rules the team system introduces across and within plants. Standardization in wages and work rules lies at the heart of the traditional labor relations system. Hourly pay standardization came only after the UAW had fought long and hard in the late 1940s and early 1950s to remove geographic differentials and incentive pay. And yet pay for knowledge, by allowing pay to vary as a function of the number of tasks mastered by a worker, will introduce variation across workers within a plant and potentially also allows for the emergence of significant variation across workers in different plants as a function of differences in the form or administration of the pay-for-knowledge system. Certainly where some plants have pay for knowledge and others do not, hourly pay for workers who perform roughly comparable jobs will vary.[17]

In one plant I visited, these sorts of problems had developed regarding the pay-for-knowledge system. Shortly after introduction of the system, workers in some areas of the plant started complaining about the varying pace at which workers had progressed up the levels of the pay-for-knowledge ladder across the teams. These workers resented that pay progression had been faster in an area of the plant that traditionally had relatively low status and in the past was a department that workers bid out of on accumulating seniority. This problem has led management and labor to monitor closely and somewhat standardize pay progression across the teams.

Even more substantial variation is likely to arise in work rules if the use of teams were to flourish for the essence of the team system is to allow and even encourage each work team to derive independent solutions to its own work responsibilities. The result is likely to be significant differences in production standards, job responsibilities, and work patterns across work groups within a plant and across plants.

In the long run the most difficult task for the union may be managing the divergence in work conditions that arise within a given plant operating on the team basis. The traditional labor relations system did not provide for perfect standardization in work conditions within or across plants so this is not an entirely new problem for the union. Yet it would appear that under the team system, this problem may become of major importance. In terms of how the local union might best be able to manage this diversity, the critical issue may be the extent to which union officials are able to use their activity on the planning committee to regulate team actions. Like the question of whether the use of teams increases or decreases union power, the union leadership's ability to maintain an active oversight role in the team system will be of critical importance.

The team system leads to a complicated interaction between enhanced worker participation and changes in traditional work rules. Consequently the use of teams confronts the union with the challenge of deciding whether it is prepared to accept worker participation if it comes along with major changes in work organization and work rules. The team system thereby also challenges the union to rethink the basis of its support for QWL type programs.

Problems for Management
For almost every problem or choice the union faces with regard to teams, there is an analogous issue confronting management. For example, some union officials oppose the use of teams because they fear a loss of personal power in the team system. The same issue arises for management. The fact that first-line supervisors often resist worker participation programs because they fear a loss of power and want to avoid the ambiguity associated with their required new role has been widely discussed in the research literature (Walton and Schlesinger 1979; Klein 1983). My field interviews suggest that this problem extends through management ranks and may impede the wider expansion of teams and QWL-type programs in the auto industry.

Management saw many advantages to the stability and standardization the traditional labor relations system provided. If team-type systems were to expand and produce a diversity in pay and work rules, management will face a difficult task in coping with this diversity. One of the problems for management will be ensuring that the union does not use the team system to win particularly favorable pay or work rules adopted in one plant and then go on to whipsaw management into accepting these favorable work conditions in other plants.

Much of the existing discussion of managerial resistance to cooperative programs may have missed an even more important issue: the
possibility that in the union sector management will come to resist
major workplace reforms because they succeed, not because they
fail.[18] Currently GM management appears to be anxious to expand
the use of teams. Yet it is unclear if this attraction to the use of teams
will persist. To date there exists relatively little experience with team
and other extensive work reorganizations in unionized settings. As a
result it is unclear what would actually happen in a case like the auto
industry where the union is an active partner to the programs. My
guess is that management in the long run might find the team system
more threatening than the union. If a team type of labor relations
system were to take hold fully it would inevitably lead to extensive
worker and union involvement in business decision making regarding work design and the implementation of new technologies. Is
management prepared to accept full-fledged worker and union participation in those decisions? If the operating team system flourishes
within GM, we may get an answer to that question.

Summary

The team system has not eliminated conflict or fundamental differences in the interests between labor and management. Labor and
management in the team plants still disagree over direct distributive
issues such as wage levels and also disagree at times over such basic
issues as seniority rights, production standards, and transfer rights.[19]
Nor is labor always satisfied with the information that management
provides regarding future production schedules or new technologies.

The team system, however, does appear to provide a process that
links innovative work rules and work organization to worker participation. Consider how some of the problems that arose in the plant
with the piecemeal participation process described earlier are dealt
with in the operating team system. In the piecemeal system workers
are reluctant to agree to further work rule changes for fear that the

erosion of the traditional job classification and seniority system would pass too much unregulated control to management. In the operating team system it is the fact that workers receive information about upcoming changes and have a right to influence those decisions through participation in the team meetings that provides a partial substitute for the security relinquished through abandonment of the traditional contract rules. Furthermore local union officials in the operating team plants receive extensive information from management regarding upcoming business decisions. In this role the local unions function somewhat the same under the piecemeal and team participation processes. The difference is that in the team plants, this exchange of information extends down to the level of hourly employees and is institutionalized through the team meetings.

Another advantage of the team system is its removal of any artificial separation between work rule issues and worker participation processes. This has facilitated the creation of bargains that cut across various issues and thereby allowed the kinds of compromises that are more difficult to achieve where collective bargaining and participation programs have been kept separate. The use of teams also relieves the local union of the need to justify the overlap between worker participation processes and the modification of work rules.

There are three paths cooperative programs in the auto industry might take in the future. Conceivably the cooperative programs will decline with the emergence of difficult contract negotiations concerning wages or other distributive bargaining issues. Or the programs may decline because of the accumulation of plant-level resistance on the part of either labor or management to the programs.

Alternatively cooperative programs may persist but only as a supplement to collective bargaining. In this case the traditional labor relations system would continue, with the cooperative programs supplementing the mainstream bargaining agenda by addressing housekeeping issues and functioning as a form of suggestion program.

Another possibility is that the cooperative programs will expand to the point that they involve a type of team system and include fundamental changes in work organization. This would lead to a basic alteration in the industry's labor relations system and inevitably would entail changes in all three of the key features of that system.

| 5 | Quantitative Assessment of the Relationship between Plant-Level Industrial Relations Performance and Economic Performance and the Impact of QWL Programs |

Does the conduct and performance of industrial relations affect the economic performance of the auto industry? And if better industrial relations performance leads to higher productivity, how large is the impact? The answers to these questions are of critical importance because they will affect the success of any strategic response by the U.S. automobile industry to heightened international competition.

This chapter sheds light on these questions by analyzing the interaction between plant-level industrial relations and economic performance in two divisions of GM.[1] The analysis utilizes annual plant-level quantitative data from the two divisions covering the 1970s. The data provide a test of the relationship between economic and industrial relations performance by indicating the extent to which plants that have relatively better industrial relations performance also have better economic performance. Analysis of the data thereby clarifies how much improvements in plant-level industrial relations are likely to improve plant-level economic performance.

The data also include measures of the QWL programs underway in these two divisions over the 1970s. These data are used to assess the longitudinal impacts of QWL programs on the labor productivity and product quality in these plants. The QWL activities underway in the two divisions during this period include quality circles; informal meetings of plant managers, workers, and union officials; and other forms of enhanced communication between labor and management. There were no major work rule concessions, team forms of work organization, or other major system changes in these plants over the period from which the data are drawn. Consequently analysis of QWL impacts in this period provides a test of the strategy by which QWL programs enter as a limited supplement to collective bargaining. It is also a strategy by which management tries to respond to intensified foreign competition by improving the tenor of labor-management relations while maintaining the key features of the traditional labor relations system.

Theoretical Model

The statistical analyses reported in this chapter follow an underlying theoretical model that hypothesizes that plant-level industrial relations and economic performance are influenced by a range of environmental economic and social factors. In this model contract negotiation and administration in each plant are assumed to influence the attitudes and behaviors of workers and managers, which in turn shape the industrial relations performance of the plant. Variations in the outcomes and performance of the plant's industrial relations processes and procedures are expected to influence plant-level economic performance through their effects on labor costs, productivity, and product quality. QWL efforts are viewed in this model as programs designed to change worker attitudes and behaviors so as to improve both the industrial relations and economic performance of the plant.

Data and Analysis Plan

The data are from eighteen plants covering the years 1970 through 1979 in division A and twenty-five plants covering 1978 through 1980 in division B. The data are annual plant averages of variables measuring the industrial relations and economic performance of each plant and a few environmental variables affecting plant performance. Within each respective division the technology and product are similar across the plants, although the technologies and products in the two divisions are different. All of the hourly workers in these plants were UAW members.

Four of the plants in division A do not report data prior to 1971. Thus the overall data set provides a pooled cross-section sample of 176 observations for division A and 75 observations for division B for most of the industrial relations and economic performance measures. Missing data reduce this sample in some of the analyses.

Industrial Relations Performance Measures

Four interrelated dimensions of plant-level industrial relations performance are measured by the data: (1) the attitudinal climate as measured by an attitude survey, (2) the results of the contract administration processes as measured by the rate of grievances and the rate of discipline cases, (3) the intensity of contract negotiations as measured by the number of demands introduced in local contract negotiations and the length of time required to reach local agreements, and (4) individual behavior as measured by the rate of absenteeism and participation in suggestion programs in the plant. Although these are not exhaustive measures of industrial relations performance at the plant level, they do cut across key aspects of the collective bargaining relationship: the negotiation of new contracts, the administration of the agreement, the attitudinal climate, and the behavior of individual workers.

The industrial relations performance measures and their respective variable names and availability are:

1. The number of grievances filed per one hundred workers. (Grievance)

2. The number of disciplinary actions per one hundred workers. The number of verbal warnings, disciplinary leaves, and discharges assessed in division A. The number of actions involving a suspension or some more severe penalty in division B. (Discipline)

3. The number of demands submitted by the union in triannual local contract negotiations. These local agreements supplement the company-wide national contract. Four rounds of bargaining (1970, 1973,

1976, 1979) occurred in the 1970s. Given that only one bargaining round occurred during the years for which data are available from division B, this variable is not included in the division B analysis. (Demands)

4. The number of days it took to reach a settlement in local contract negotiations before (negative) or after (positive) settlement of the company agreement. These data are available only for division A. (Negotiation time)

5. A survey asked salaried employees (including first-line supervisors) a number of questions. In division A the questions focused on the state of labor-management relations. The higher the survey score, the more cooperative the relations. In this division a summary score of the questions for each plant for the years 1976–1979 is available. In division B the questions concerned the perceived quality of compensation benefit levels, work environment, relationships with supervisors and subordinates, and career progress. In division B the variable is the percentage of respondents in each plant having an overall survey score greater than 3.2 on a 1 to 5 scale. (Attitude)

6. The percentage of employees who submitted at least one suggestion during the year in the voluntary suggestion program. Available only for division B. (Sugpct)

7. The absentee rate as a percentage of straight time hours, excluding contractual days off. (Absentee)

Economic Performance Measures

The economic performance of each plant is assessed by two measures of direct labor efficiency and product quality:

1. A quality index derived from a count of the number of faults and demerits appearing in inspections of the product. A higher quality score is associated with better product quality. In division A this index is available only for 1973–1979. (Quality)

2. A direct labor efficiency index comparing the actual hours of direct labor input to standardized hours calculated by industrial engineers at GM. The labor standards used in this index are adjusted for differences in product attributes. A higher direct labor efficiency index is associated with higher efficiency and lower costs. (Direct)

QWL Program Measures

With the cooperation of the UAW, GM began to implement QWL programs in its plants in 1973, though the actual development of QWL programs among salaried and hourly employees varied widely across plants. Starting in 1977 each plant in division A reported annually to its division headquarters on the QWL efforts underway in the plant. The measure of the intensity of the QWL effort in division A used here is derived from a content analysis of these reports and therefore is available only for the years 1977 through 1979; it is labeled QWLRAT.[2] In division B the extent of QWL development is measured by the percentage of hourly employees involved in some form of QWL activity in each plant. These figures are annual estimates provided by the personnel director in each plant and are labeled QWLINVHR. The QWL activities in both divisions include quality circles and other forms of improved communication between labor and management but not more radical changes in work rules or work organization. The limited scope of the programs in division A is indicated by the representative list of QWL activities reported in the appendix to this chapter.

Environmental Measures

A number of economic and social factors influence plant-level industrial relations and economic performance, including the demographic characteristics of the work force, the size of the plant, and how close the plant is operating to full capacity. The available data set measures the influence of the business cycle and the degree of capacity utilization with a measure of the annual number of overtime hours divided by the number of straight-time hours worked by all production workers (Overtime ratio). The plant size is measured with the total annual work hours of all production workers in division A and the average number of hourly workers in division B (Work Force).

These data measure only some of the relevant theoretical determinants of plant-level industrial relations and economic performance. Of all the environmental and organizational variables that could be measured, limits are imposed here by the data available from company files and reports. Although these data are exceedingly rich and informative, they do not incorporate all of the potentially important sources of variation. For example, turnover of top plant management or union leadership, internal union and management political characteristics, and differences in the technology and skill mix in the plant may affect industrial relations and economic performance. In the regression analyses for division A, dummy variables are utilized to try to capture some of these unmeasured plant specific effects.

The analysis starts with a description of the overall patterns and variations in the industrial relations and economic performance outcomes across the plants. Then the intercorrelations between the industrial relations performance indicators and the correlations between economic performance, industrial relations performance, and environmental variables are reviewed. Finally the impact of the QWL programs are assessed.

Interplant Variations

Table 5.1 reports descriptive statistics for division A in 1979; table 5.2 reports similar figures for division B in 1980. These figures show that despite the common technology union, and employer from which these data are drawn, there is wide variation across the plants within each division in grievance rates, discipline rates, and other industrial relations performance indicators. For example, in 1979 in division A

Table 5.1
Industrial relations and economic performance in 1979, division A

	Mean	Minimum	Maximum	Standard Deviation
Grievance	124.3	24.5	450.2	133.1
Absentee	7.4	4.7	10.3	1.7
Discipline	44.5	20.0	86.8	17.5
Demands	364.6	102	754	196.4
Negotiation time	76.8	−110	532	143.4
Attitude	2.9	2.2	3.8	.5
Quality	127.6	122.0	137.0	3.7
Direct labor	87.4	57.1	103.7	13.2

Table 5.2
Industrial relations and economic performance in 1980, division B

Variable	Mean	Minimum Value	Maximum Value	Standard Deviation
Grievance	45.9	5.5	121.1	25.7
Absentee	6.3	4.6	8.8	1.1
Discipline	4.5	.9	15.4	3.2
Attitude	54.4	40	74	7.9
Sugpct	17.8	8.0	37.3	7.6
Direct Labor	−.2	−23.7	20.4	9.6
Quality	129.3	119.0	140.0	6.8
Percentage hourly QWL involvement	15.7	0	72.4	24.2

grievances per hundred workers varied from a low of 24.5 in one plant to a high of 450.2 in another plant. Absenteeism varied between 4.7 and 10.3 percent. The number of contract demands introduced in local negotiations for the 1979 local agreements varied from a low of 102 to a high of 754.

The same variation in industrial performance is found in division B. For example, in 1980 the grievance rate is 5.5 per hundred workers in one plant and 121.2 in another plant. The percentage of workers participating in suggestion programs varies in division B from 8.0 percent in one plant to 37.3 percent in another plant.[3]

The economic significance of the variation in the indexes of economic
performance is not as easily interpreted since these indexes are a
product of GM's particular accounting and quality control systems;
however, these figures also show considerable variation around their
means. For instance, direct labor efficiency varies between 57.1 percent of standards in one plant to 103.7 percent of standards in another
plant in division A. In division B the annual product quality index is
119.0 in one plant and 140.0 in another plant.

Time plots of the data reveal that an important source of variation
appears to be correspondence to the business cycle and the volume of
work in the plants. The annual mean grievance rate, absentee rate,
quality index, and direct labor index for division A are plotted in
figures 5.1 and 5.2. As illustrated, there are increases in grievance
activity and absenteeism and declines in direct labor efficiency during
the growth years of 1970 through 1973 followed by opposite move-

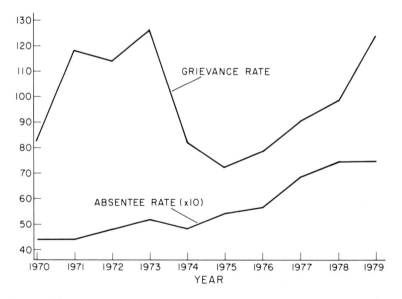

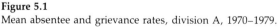

Figure 5.1
Mean absentee and grievance rates, division A, 1970–1979.

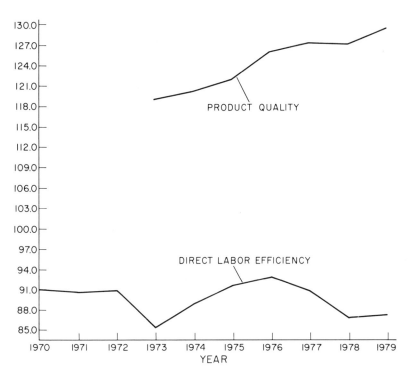

Figure 5.2
Mean direct labor efficiency and product quality indexes, division A, 1970–1979.

ments in these measures as the oil embargo and the consequent decline in auto sales took hold between 1973 and 1975. As the industry
recovered from 1976 through 1979, grievance activity and absenteeism again rose and direct labor efficiency fell substantially. These
plots also reveal an upward time trend in the quality index and
absentee rate over the 1970s.

Relationships between Industrial Relations Performance Measures

The correlations among the measures of industrial relations performance across plants and years in divisions A and B are reported in
tables 5.3 and 5.4. The figures show a high degree of intercorrelation
among the various measures. For instance, the data show a strong

Table 5.3
Interrelationships among industrial relations performance variables as measured by
simple correlation coefficients, division A

	Attitude	Grievance	Discipline	Absentee	Demands	Negotiation Time
Attitude	1.00					
Grievance	−.77[a]	1.00				
Discipline	−.20	.44[a]	1.00			
Absentee	−.49[a]	.26[a]	.43[a]	1.00		
Demands	−.49[a]	.31[a]	.31[a]	.31[a]	1.00	
Negotiation time	−.52[a]	.57[a]	.30[a]	.16	.17	1.00

Note: Number of observations ranges between 171 and 176 for correlations involving
measures of absentee, grievance, and discipline rates. Number of observations
ranges between 65 and 68 for correlations involving climate, demands, and negotiation time.
a. Statistically significant at .01 level.

Table 5.4
Interrelationships among industrial relations performance variables as measured by
simple correlation coefficients, division B

	Grievance	Absentee	Discipline	Attitude	Sugpct
Grievance	1.00				
Absentee	.26[a]	1.00			
Discipline	.29[b]	.41[b]	1.00		
Attitude	−.47[b]	−.48[b]	−.36[b]	1.00	
Sugpct	−.27[a]	−.13	.16	.43[a]	

Note: There are seventy-five observations.
a. Significant at .05 level.
b. Significant at .01 level.

correlation between the various indicators of conflict in the plants.
Focusing on figures from division A in table 5.3, the higher the grievance rate in a plant, the higher the discipline rate ($r = .44$), the more
demands introduced into local negotiations ($r = .31$), and the longer
the negotiating time required to reach a local agreement ($r = .57$). All
of these correlations are statistically significant at the 1 percent level.
The same pattern holds in division B as revealed in table 5.4. There,
for instance, a higher grievance rate is correlated with higher disci-

pline rates ($r = .29$); again this correlation is statistically significant at the 1 percent level.

The data also reveal a strong connection between measures of employee attitudes and behavior and indicators of the level of conflict. Looking at figures from division B in table 5.4, better attitudes among salaried personnel are associated with lower grievance rates ($r = -.47$) and lower discipline rates ($r = -.36$); both correlations are statistically significant at the 1 percent level. The connection between individual behavior and the level of conflict also is revealed in the associations that absentee rates have with grievance rates and discipline rates in division B. These interrelationships are consistent in both direction and magnitude with the interrelationships that exist between the same variables in division A reported in table 5.3.

Relationship between Industrial Relations and Economic Performance

Correlations between measures of economic performance and the industrial relations performance measures from divisions A and B are reported in tables 5.5 and 5.6. These correlations provide strong evidence that the level of conflict and individual attitudes and behavior affect economic performance. A number of the indicators of plant-level conflict intensity are strongly associated with the economic performance indicators. For example, in table 5.5 (division A) higher grievance rates are associated with lower direct labor efficiency ($r = -.49$) and poorer product quality ($r = -.27$), and these correlations are statistically significant at the 1 percent level.

The same connection between the degree of conflict and economic performance is indicated by the fact that longer negotiation time over local contracts in division A is associated with lower direct labor efficiency ($r = -.40$) and poorer product quality ($r = -.39$); again these correlations are statistically significant at the 1 percent level. A similar connection between the degree of conflict and economic per-

Table 5.5
Correlations of economic performance with industrial relations performance and
environmental factors, division A

	Quality	Direct Labor Efficiency
Grievance	$-.27^b$	$-.49^b$
Discipline	$-.20^a$	$-.35^b$
Absentee	.13	$-.38^b$
Attitude	$.44^b$	$.44^b$
Demands	$-.20$	$-.32^b$
Negotiation time	$-.39^b$	$-.40^b$
Work force	$-.05$	$-.24^b$
Overtime ratio	.05	$-.29^b$

Note: Number of observations ranges between 65 and 68 for correlations involving
climate, demands, and negotiation time. For all other variables the number of observations ranges between 126 and 176.
a. Statistically significant at .05 level.
b. Statistically significant at .01 level.

Table 5.6
Correlations of economic performance with industrial relations performance and
environmental factors, division B

	Quality	Direct Labor Efficiency
Grievance	$-.18^b$	$-.48^b$
Discipline	$.21^a$	$-.25^b$
Absentee	.05	$-.25^a$
Attitude	$.48^b$	$.40^b$
Sugpct	$.73^b$	$.38^b$
Overtime ratio	$-.40^b$	$-.28^b$
Work force	$-.33^b$	$-.31^b$

Note: The sample size is 75.
a. Statistically significant at .05 level.
b. Statistically significant at .01 level.

formance is revealed in a number of the other correlations reported
in tables 5.5 and 5.6.

A connection between individual attitudes and behavior and economic performance is revealed by the association in division B in table
5.6 between employee attitudes and higher direct labor efficiency
($r = .40$) and better product quality ($r = .48$). Similarly the greater

the participation in the suggestion program in division B, the higher the direct labor efficiency ($r = .38$) and the better the product quality ($r = .73$). All of these correlations are statistically significant at the 1 percent level and are consistent with the associations found in division A in table 5.5.

The data in tables 5.5 and 5.6 also show associations among the measured environmental variables, work force size and the overtime ratio, and economic performance measures. For example, in division B the higher the use of overtime, the lower the labor efficiency ($r = -.28$) and the poorer the product quality ($r = -.40$). Both correlations are statistically significant at the 1 percent level. In addition larger plant size is associated with lower labor efficiency and poorer product quality in both divisions, supporting the hypotheses that higher capacity utilization and larger plant work forces are associated with lower labor efficiency.

It might at first seem surprising that in this capital-intensive industry, labor efficiency declines as capacity utilization and the use of overtime increase. The point to keep in mind is that these plants rely on layoffs and changes in the number of operating shifts to adjust to output variation. Consequently there is little of the sort of labor hoarding during recessions that contributes to the opposite association between labor efficiency and output found in other industries.

Although I have no direct evidence to test this hypothesis, GM managers stated the view that the association between labor efficiency and overtime hours revealed by these data arise from the facts that younger workers are hired during upturns and have lower productivity, in part, because they require some training. Furthermore, it appears that labor productivity declines in these plants when output turns up for many of the reasons cited by Commons (1921): that labor relations become more conflictual and workers informally reduce their effort as the labor market becomes tighter during economic boom periods.[4] With regard to the association between work force size and labor efficiency, GM managers frequently stated that this reflected that larger auto plants were harder to manage and tended to generate greater conflict between labor and management.

The correlations between industrial relations and economic performance measures reported in tables 5.5 and 5.6 provide evidence of associations between these measures, but these correlations are not an adequate test of causality, for it may well be that environmental factors are simultaneously affecting both industrial relations and economic performance and thereby producing the observed correlation between industrial relations and economic performance. To test for the independent effects that industrial relations performance exert on plant-level economic performance, the influences of environmental factors must be controlled for. Regression analysis can be used to provide this test.

Pooled time series–cross-section regressions were estimated separately for divisions A and B. The regressions were estimated with direct labor efficiency and product quality as the dependent variable, with a QWL involvement measure and various industrial relations performance measures as independent variables and with the ratio of overtime hours and work force size entered as control variables.[5] Since the available data differed for the two divisions, the regression results for each will be discussed separately.

Regression Analysis of the Impact of Industrial Relations Performance on Economic Performance

Division A
Pooled time series–cross-section regressions are estimated with data from eighteen plants with annual data covering the years 1970 through 1979 from division A. Dummy variables are included in some of the regressions to control for the influence of unmeasured plant-specific factors that might otherwise bias the analysis.[6] This is equivalent to estimating a fixed-effects model.

The regression results for division A are reported in tables 5.7 and 5.8. Whenever the grievance rate is included as a control variable in the regressions reported in tables 5.7 and 5.8, higher grievance rates are associated with lower product quality and lower direct labor efficiency; these associations are statistically significant at the 1 percent level. This lends further support to the hypothesis that the level of industrial relations conflict affects plant-level economic performance.

The association between absentee rates, and product quality and direct labor efficiency in the regression analysis of division A data is not consistent. Higher absenteeism is associated with better product

Table 5.7
Regression analysis of impact of environmental, industrial relations, and QWL rating measures on product quality, division A

Explanatory Variables	Quality	Quality	Quality	Quality
Intercept	111.207[a]	116.021[a]	123.340[a]	124.049[a]
	(3.149)	(2.372)	(1.548)	(1.226)
Overtime ratio	.082	.101	.049	.048
	(.078)	(.084)	(.082)	(.082)
Work force	−.132	−.122	−.184	−.272
	(.334)	(.318)	(.178)	(.181)
Grievance	−.027		−.019[a]	
	(.009)		(.005)	
Absentee	1.167[a]		.320	
	(.330)		(.260)	
QWL rating	.183[a]	.281[a]	.240[a]	.267[a]
	(.056)	(.054)	(.059)	(.060)
Plant dummies	Included[b]	Included[b]		
R^2	.606	.529	.231	.153
F	7.20	5.89	7.23	7.35
n	126	126	126	126

Note: Standard errors are in parentheses.
a. Statistically significant at .01 level, two-tailed test.
b. As a set statistically significant at .01 level.

Table 5.8
Regression analysis of impact of environmental, industrial relations, and QWL
rating measures on direct labor efficiency, division A.

Explanatory Variables	Direct	Direct	Direct	Direct
Intercept	126.305[b]	127.272[b]	96.949[b]	103.815[b]
	(5.387)	(3.829)	(2.316)	(2.078)
Overtime ratio	−.053	−.006	−.114	−.349[a]
	(.133)	(.136)	(.130)	(.143)
Work force	−.099	−.619	−.001	−.347
	(.533)	(.496)	(.278)	(.312)
Grievance	−.047[b]		−.050[b]	
	(.014)		(.008)	
Absentee	.567		−1.336[b]	
	(.550)		(.410)	
QWL rating	−.153	−.050	−.039	−.021
	(.105)	(.095)	(.103)	(.111)
Plant dummies	Included[c]	Included[c]		
R^2	.549	5.08	.320	.093
F	8.19	7.78	15.55	5.73
n	171	171	171	171

Note: Standard errors are in parentheses.
a. Statistically significant at .05 level, two-tailed test.
b. Statistically significant at .01 level, two-tailed test.
c. As a set statistically significant at .01 level.

quality, and in one of the regressions this association is statistically
significant at the 1 percent level (table 5.7); however, this may merely
reflect the concomitant rise in both quality and absenteeism plotted
in figures 5.2 and 5.3.[7] In one of the regressions, higher direct labor efficiency is associated with lower absentee rates at a statistically significant level of 1 percent, though in another regression this
association is reversed and is not statistically significant (table 5.8).

Whenever they are included in the regressions, the plant dummy
variables are statistically significant at the 1 percent level as a group.[8]
This indicates there are a number of unmeasured plant characteristics
affecting economic performance.

Division B

Table 5.9 reports the results of pooled time series–cross-section regressions using annual data from the twenty-five plants in division B for the years 1978 through 1980. In contrast to the regressions for division A, in these regressions all of the available industrial relations performance measures are included in the regression. The correlations in table 5.4 show a high degree of intercorrelation among the various industrial relations performance measures. In the face of this intercorrelation the coefficients on the individual industrial relations measures will not provide a good test of the composite effects of

Table 5.9
Regression analysis of impact of environmental, industrial relations, and hourly QWL involvement measures on direct labor efficiency and product quality, division B

Explanatory Variables	(1) Direct	(2) Direct	(3) Quality	(4) Quality
Intercept	− 16.528	9.062	109.490	139.202
Overtime ratio	28.729	− 10.944	− 22.893	57.825[a]
	(30.991)	(28.705)	(18.612)	(20.959)
Work force	.022	− .320[a]	.0002	− .002[a]
	(.130)	(.079)	(.0007)	(.0006)
Grievance	− .054		.0002	
	(.039)		(.0003)	
Discipline	− .077[a]		− .0002	
	(.029)		(.0002)	
Absentee	.411		.005	
	(.650)		(.004)	
Attitude	.349[a]		.130	
	(.154)		(.093)	
Sugpct	.028		.007[a]	
	(.230)		(.001)	
QWLInvHr	− .023	.019	.0001	.0002
	(.042)	(.043)	(.00005)	(.0003)
R^2	.467	.242	.675	.310
F	6.014	6.369	14.272	9.001
n	64	64	64	64

Note: Standard errors are in parentheses.
a. Statistically significant at the .01 level, two-tailed test.

industrial relations performance on labor efficiency or product quality. The combined effects of the industrial relations performance measures can be assessed by comparing the R^2 when estimating an equation with and without all of the industrial relations performance measures included as control variables in the equation. To provide this test in some of the estimated equations reported in table 5.9, the industrial relations performance measures are not included in the equation as control variables.

The regression reported in column 1 in table 5.9 shows a statistically significant (.01 level) impact of discipline rates and attitudes on direct labor efficiency. The regression in column 3 shows a statistically significant (.01 level) impact of participation in suggestion programs on product quality.

A large cumulative impact of industrial relations performance on direct labor efficiency in division B is indicated by the fact that the R^2 rises from .242 (column 2) to .467 (column 1) when the industrial relations variables are added to the direct labor regression. This is a statistically significant (.01 level) effect, $F = 4.64$. Similarly the industrial relations variables have a strong cumulative impact on product quality. The R^2 rises from .310 when the industrial relations variables are not in the quality regression (column 4) to .675 when they are included in the regression (column 3).

These results are consistent with the correlations reported in table 5.6 and provide strong evidence that plant-level industrial relations performance affects plant-level economic performance.

QWL Evaluation

A number of problems make QWL evaluation difficult. One arises from the pattern of QWL program diffusion and is referred to in the economics literature as selection bias. The selection problem arises from the fact that plants already having better industrial relations and economic performance may well be more likely to develop more extensive QWL programs. Given that measurement of better performance is imprecise in the available data, in the face of this diffusion pattern it is difficult to distinguish between whether better-performing plants develop more QWL or the fact that the development of more extensive QWL programs in a plant produces better industrial relations and economic performance. One way to cope with this and other problems is to use a number of methods to test for the impacts of QWL programs and then look for consistent results in the various methods. Following are presented the results from two different approaches to the assessment of QWL program impacts.

Changes in High and Low QWL Plants in Division A

The industrial relations and economic performance of the five plants with the highest and lowest QWL program rating in division A before and after 1977 are compared in table 5.10. The comparison is made before and after 1977 because discussion with the QWL staff in this division suggest that although the QWL effort formally began in 1973, it was not until 1977 that QWL programs actually were underway in any form in most of the plants.

Table 5.10
Comparison of change in economic and industrial relations performance in five plants with highest and lowest QWL 1977 program rating, division A

	1974–1976		1977–1979	
Percentage Change in	Five Plants with Highest QWL 1977 Rating	Five Plants with Lowest QWL 1977 Rating	Five Plants with Highest QWL 1977 Rating	Five Plants with Lowest QWL 1977 Rating
Quality	4.2	6.1	1.5	− 0.2
Direct labor	5.5	4.7	−2.4	− 4.8
Grievance	17.6	4.3	5.2	4.8
Absentee	47.5	23.4	1.8	20.6
Discipline	42.1	18.8	6.0	11.5

As the figures show, from 1974 to 1976, except for direct labor efficiency, measures of the mean industrial relations and economic performance of the plants that later developed high levels of QWL activity and high QWL program ratings were deteriorating relative to the performance of the five plants that later had low QWL program ratings. For instance, in the plants with high QWL program ratings, from 1974 to 1976 grievance and absentee rates rose 17.6 percent and 47.5 percent on average, while in the plants with low QWL program ratings, grievance and absentee rates rose 4.3 percent and 23.4 percent.

In contrast, from 1977 to 1979 mean industrial relations and economic performance measures were improving in the five plants with high QWL ratings in comparison with the five plants with low QWL ratings (except for grievance rates). The plants with highest QWL ratings on average had a 1.5 percent improvement in their quality index, while the plants with lowest QWL ratings had a .2 percent decrease in their quality index. With respect to absentee rates over the 1977 through 1979 period, the plants with the most QWL activity had a 1.8 percent increase, while the five lowest-ranked plants had a 20.6 percent increase. This suggests that the QWL programs had positive, though fairly marginal, effects on industrial relations and economic performance in this division.

Within the top and bottom groups, however, there was wide variation among plants in changes in industrial relations and economic performance. None of the differences in the changes in performance from 1977 to 1979 between the top and bottom five plants are statistically significant at even the .10 level.

The regressions reported in tables 5.7 and 5.8 provide another test of the impacts of QWL programs.[9] These regressions test for the effects that QWL programs in division A had on labor efficiency and product quality after controlling for the influence of work force size and the use of overtime and other factors measured by the plant dummy variables. Given the unavailability of measures of the intensity of QWL programs prior to 1977, in these regressions a score of zero for the QWL program rating (QWLRAT) is entered for each plant for each year prior to 1977. Undoubtedly this introduces some measurement error, but this procedure has the advantage of allowing the use of other plant characteristics (environmental and industrial relations) prior to 1977 as controls in the estimation.

In table 5.7 the sign of the coefficients on QWL rating implies that more intensive QWL programs are associated with better product quality. In all four regressions the coefficients on QWL rating are statistically significant at the 1 percent level. When the grievance and absentee rates are not included as control variables, the coefficient on QWL rating is higher and has a higher T statistic. This suggests that some of the positive impact of the QWL programs on quality is transmitted through the impact of QWL on grievance and absentee rates.

In table 5.8 the negative sign of the coefficients on QWL rating when direct labor efficiency is the dependent variable implies that more intensive QWL programs are associated with lower efficiency and higher labor costs; however, none of these coefficients is statistically significant at even the 10 percent level. This is also inconsistent with the figures in table 5.10 showing that in division A the five plants with high QWL ratings in 1977 had relatively lower declines in their direct labor efficiency during the 1977–1979 economic upturn.

Growth of QWL Participation in Division B

Hourly employee involvement in QWL programs in division B diffused at a very slow rate. Hourly employee QWL involvement rose slowly from 5.0 percent in 1973 (the year the QWL programs started) to 9.5 percent in 1979 and then increased to 15.7 percent in 1980. This is consistent with the information gathered in the plant visits discussed in chapter 4. QWL growth accelerated only when the auto industry underwent a sharp economic downturn after 1979 that led to a large number of layoffs and led labor and management to search more aggressively for alterations in labor relations that might assist the recovery of the industry.

As of 1980 six plants in division B had at least 33 percent of their hourly employees involved in some form of QWL program. In 1980 nine plants in the division had no QWL hourly employee involvement, and the remaining plants had very few hourly employees involved.

The regressions reported in table 5.9 provide an estimate of the impact of QWL involvement on industrial relations performance and economic performance during the period 1978 to 1980 in division B. QWL program intensity is measured by the percentage of the hourly work force in each plant (in each year) involved in some form of QWL activity.

When either direct labor efficiency or product quality is the dependent variable, there is no measured statistically significant impact of hourly QWL involvement. Even when the industrial relations variables are excluded, in both the direct labor and quality equations, the coefficient on QWL hourly employee involvement is small and statistically insignificant (columns 2 and 4), suggesting that the QWL programs underway in this division over the 1970s had no impact on plant-level economic performance.

Summary of Data Analysis

Overall the data provide strong evidence of an association between the plant-level industrial relations and economic performance. There are strong and consistent correlations between the industrial relations and economic performance in both divisions. The regressions analysis indicates that the association between industrial relations and economic performance is causal. The regressions show that in division A lower plant grievance rates are associated in a statistically significant manner with higher labor efficiency and better product quality. In division B the industrial relations measures have a large and statistically significant cumulative impact on labor efficiency and product quality.

This points to the conclusion that where labor and management are able to reduce the level of labor-management conflict in a plant and create more positive attitudes among the work force, these improvements affect the plant's labor costs and product quality. Another indicator of this is the fact that the descriptive statistics reported in tables 5.1 and 5.2 reveal wide variation in labor efficiency and product quality across these plants. This variation occurs even in the face of similar technologies, union, and management structure.

It would be difficult to explain the measured divergence in industrial relations and economic performance if one held to the view that economic forces rapidly move production systems to their most economically efficient point. One could try to argue that the wide divergence in economic performance across these plants is a product of unmeasured differences in technology or short-run perturbations. I do not find these explanations convincing in the face of the consistently wide scope of the differences in performance across these plants. Rather I interpret the data as supporting the claim that economic forces do not move production systems rapidly to their most efficient point.[10] The divergence across these plants suggests that the steps and strategies adopted by management and labor at the plant level have a sizable impact on economic outcomes.

The wide divergence in the industrial relations indicators across these plants points to the fact that there exists a sizable variation in the tenor and outputs of labor-management relations across GM's plants. A clear indication of the magnitude of the variation is the fact that the grievance rates vary by as much of a factor of 20 across plants in the same division even though the structure of the grievance procedures in these plants is identical since all follow the guidelines of the national GM-UAW contract.

The plants in division A or B that have relatively low grievance and absentee rates and relatively better labor efficiency and product quality do so while operating with the traditional features of the auto labor relations system. None of these plants during the period of the 1970s had major work rule concessions or team forms of work organization or any other major system changes. Of course, it cannot be assumed that all of the measured relative advantages of the best-performing plants in these divisions (40 percent in direct labor efficiency) could be easily copied and transferred to the poorer-performing plants. Some of the advantage may be due to personalities or long-standing cultural and historical factors. Yet a significant fraction of the variation may well be under the direct control of labor and management. The correlations between industrial performance measures and the economic performance variables suggest that this may be the case.

The wide variation in the tenor of labor-management relations across GM's plants and the connection between industrial relations and economic performance highlight a potential strategy the parties at GM and other companies might pursue in response to the heightened competition and cost pressure facing the U.S. auto industry. The strategy would be to try to improve overall economic performance by bringing up the performance of the poorer-performing plants to the level of performance attained in the better-performing plants. This is a rather limited strategy. The strategy is limited because it does not entail changes in any of the key features of the traditional auto labor relations system. Rather the objective would be to improve the tenor of labor-management relations while maintaining the existing rules, procedures, and bargaining patterns that have traditionally structured the relationship.

QWL programs that maintain a limited focus and function as a supplement to the traditional labor relations system could be part of this strategy. The statistical data provide some evidence that this sort of QWL program can have modest positive effects on industrial relations and economic performance.[11] For example, the before- and after-1977 group comparisons in division A suggest that the QWL programs there had some positive impact on absentee and grievance rates and on product quality. The regression analysis also showed positive impacts of the QWL programs on product quality in division A, although the regression analysis for division B shows no impact of the QWL programs underway between 1978 and 1980 on plant-level economic performance.

Overall the measured impacts of the QWL programs underway in the two divisions over the 1970s are fairly modest. Yet with modest objectives, QWL programs could play a useful role as part of an effort to improve economic performance by raising the industrial relations performance of the poorer-performing plants up to the level attained by the best plants in GM. At the same time the statistical evidence reviewed in this chapter suggests that attempts to achieve more significant improvements in economic performance would have to be more extensive and include changes in the key features that structure the auto labor relations system. The next chapter explores the likelihood and form of alternative future paths that include such major changes to the auto industry's labor relations system.

Appendix
The QWL Content Analysis, Division A

The QWL content analysis was performed in the following manner. Cards that listed the representative QWL activities below were provided to five industrial relations professors and graduate students with expertise in QWL programs, who were asked to rank these activities in three categories according to the significance they attached to the activity. The three categories then were assigned the following weights: minor significance, 1 point; intermediate significance, 2 points; and major significance, 3 points. An average weight was derived for each activity based on the rankings provided by the five experts. Another expert then recorded the occurrence of these activities in each plant by using plant managers' annual reports that describe the QWL activities within each plant. Each activity was assigned its weight, and a total QWL score was computed for each plant for each year (1977–1979). In a test of the reliabiity of this scoring procedure, a second expert also reviewed the annual reports and assigned the appropriate weight. The correlation between the scores obtained by the two experts was .85.

List of Representative QWL Activities

1. Open house and plant tours for employee families or community residents, or both.

2. Community relations projects such as blood drives or United Way campaigns.

3. Physical plant improvements, such as painting the walls or housekeeping improvements.

4. Off-site training or problem discussion meetings with salaried staff.

5. Off-site training or problem discussion meetings with hourly workers.

6. Off-site meetings between plant management and union representatives.

7. Alcohol- or drug-abuse programs.

8. Experimental projects that involve specific work groups in the plant.

9. Promotional programs that advertise the plant, such as plant T-shirts, jackets, or pens.

10. Consultation meetings with hourly workers or union representatives over future QWL initiatives.

11. Formation (or continuation) of a union-management QWL or other committee.

12. Use of an outside consultant (or a GM or UAW QWL specialist).

13. Special programs emphasizing product quality, offering such rewards as prizes, cash, or recognition.

14. Motivational films or other media presentations to the work force.

15. Feedback of QWL survey to workers or union representatives, or both.

16. Joint GM-UAW orientation programs for new hires.

17. Management's sharing information on plans for plant expansion, renovation, or other changes with workers or union representatives, or both.

18. Upward communications programs, such as question boxes, suggestion boxes, or plant newsletters.

19. Special dinners or luncheons for, for example, retiring employees, Christmas, or other occasions.

20. Enhancing the role of the first-line supervisors, such as through special seminars.

The Future Course of U.S.
Auto Labor Relations

What is likely to happen to the U.S. auto labor relations system in the years ahead? Will the dominance of the three key features of the traditional system reemerge? Or will worker participation and work organization reforms expand to the point that a fundamentally new labor relations system emerges?

The history of auto bargaining shows that environmental factors have shaped the labor relations system. The steady adherence to wage rules from 1948 until 1979 was supported by the industry's long-run growth in sales and employment. The connective bargaining structure, in turn, was feasible given the low level of import sales and the complete unionization of the Big Three, which produced an overlap between labor and product markets in the industry. The steady growth in autoworkers' earnings and Big Three profits also contributed to the acceptability on both sides of the bargaining table for the continuation of a job control focus. It was only the sharp economic slump after 1979 that led to significant modifications in the traditional auto labor relations system.

The central role of the economic environment in shaping the choices before labor and management implies that future economic developments must be assessed to arrive at predictions regarding the future course of auto labor relations. Yet the history of auto bargaining also reveals that labor and management retained a degree of strategic choice in the design of the labor relations system. The bargaining system that emerged out of the instability of the immediate post–

World War II period had to be consistent with the economic environment, but the system was not strictly determined by environmental factors. Thus in terms of future developments, even in the face of any given set of environmental pressures, labor and management will exercise some independent control over the course taken in the conduct of labor relations. This suggests the need to consider the likely strategic choices of those parties.

Environmental Economic Pressures

Recent changes in the economics of the auto industry have generated the need for greater flexibility in the production system and cost moderation. The question of relevance regarding future developments is the extent to which these or other economic pressures will be significant in the future. One can get a sense of the future importance of these pressures by analyzing the factors contributing to each.

Pressure for Increased Flexibility
Three factors contribute to the need for more flexibility in the auto production and labor relations systems: product markets, new technologies, and macroeconomic events.

In the late 1970s U.S. car producers appeared to move away from the strategy of providing a wide range of vehicle types, a product strategy characteristic of the Big Three over the postwar period. Rather the Big Three increasingly appear to be targeting their product lines toward a specialty or niche market strategy (Altshuler et al. 1984, chap. 11). In part this shift is a consequence of the fact that the U.S. companies hold a competitive advantage increasing only in the larger car end of the world auto market. A contributing factor to this development was the success of the Japanese in capturing the small car market and the more recent upscale movement of Japanese producers into the mid-size market. Other contributing factors inducing this shift include the rise in the price of oil, which led consumers to be more concerned with gas mileage and produced a reduction in the variation across car size lines as large car lines were made lighter and smaller.

The inability to compete with Japanese producers in the small car market has led U.S. companies largely to abandon that end of the market. This trend is illustrated by GM's recent product strategy. In 1982 GM announced plans to halt production of the Chevette and in the future will rely on imports of the S car from Spain, imports of small and minicars made by Isuzu and Suzuki in Japan, and small cars jointly produced by GM and Toyota in a plant in California to supply the small car market.[1] The remaining domestic production of GM has become increasingly centered around the production of high-priced specialty vehicles. These include sport cars (Fiero, Corvette), recreation vehicles (sport vans), and other specialty type vehicles (mini-vans, convertibles, sport coupes). Other U.S. firms similarly have moved toward foreign production of small cars with domestic production to be focused around high-priced and specialty vehicles.

Changes in the U.S. producers' product strategy appears to be part of the worldwide collapse of distinct national product markets in the auto industry. The previous sharp distinctions among U.S., European, and Japanese car markets are being replaced by a world market in which many companies produce cars of a similar type. In the words of the final report of the M.I.T. International Auto Program, in the future "every producer may come to pose a threat to every other producer in every OECD market" (Altshuler et al. 1984, p. 368). In such a market U.S. producers would have to be able to adjust quickly production types and volumes in response to the actions of other producers around the world.

This shift in product strategy has important implications for the production process because production schedules for specialty cars would be more subject to changes in consumer preferences or competitive offerings than the industry's previous product mix. Consequently on the shop floor there will be a greater need for the capacity for a rapid adjustment of production volumes and type to changing market demand.

The traditional labor relations system in the U.S. auto industry, however, appears to be poorly suited to this kind of rapid change and flexibility in the production process (Sabel 1982; Piore and Sabel 1984). One of the ways to facilitate changes in product type or the simultaneous production of a number of product lines is to have broadly trained workers who can easily shift across job tasks. But the U.S. job control system is based on the existence of a large number of narrowly defined job classifications.

The ability to shift production types rapidly is hindered further in the United States by the detailed regulation of job tasks provided in the job control system. For instance, the formal grievance procedure is geared to the careful adjudication of disputes arising out of the interpretation of the transfer and assignment rights specified in the local and national contracts. The problem is that this system slows the redeployment of labor across job tasks or product lines when changes in the production process raise issues regarding job jurisdiction. Another way to adjust the production system in order to quicken the response to product market changes is to manufacture more than one product line on a given production or assembly line. But this also requires workers and work rules that can flexibly adjust.

Consequently the greater the switch in the product strategy of U.S. producers to this specialty or niche form, or the more volatile the world product markets, the greater the pressure for labor relations changes that facilitate flexibility in the production process.

Associated with these shifts in auto product markets is the increased importance of product quality as a competitive factor (Altshuler et al. 1984). In the United States this shows up in the fact that the superior fit and trim of Japanese cars has emerged as an important determinant of car buyer decisions. Heightened worker concern for quality requires a voluntary commitment and participation in the production process on the part of workers in a manner not provided by the traditional hierarchical and job control orientation of U.S. shop floor labor relations. This has added to the need for more flexible and participatory forms of labor relations and work organization.

The increased use of robotic and microelectronic technology will provide an additional push for more flexible work rules. Robotic and other microelectronic technology allow rapid adjustments in production mix. The flexibility to switch product types appears to be the critical advantage robotics have over earlier forms of automation. Therefore the greater the shift to a more volatile and uncertain product market, the greater the need for such technologies.[2] A machine that is frequently reprogrammed, however, or an assembly line that is frequently rearranged requires workers and work rules that flexibly adjust. Consequently these technologies require more rapid switches in job tasks and broader job assignments than commonly occur in the traditional production system.

One of the more direct effects of increased robotization is to shift the composition of the laboring work force away from unskilled production workers and toward skilled tradesmen who perform the repair and setup work associated with the new technology. Reflecting past increases in the level of automation, the share of skilled tradesmen gradually increased in the major auto companies from around 15 percent in the mid-1930s to about 22 percent by 1980 and is forecast to increase steadily.[3]

One of the potential future effects of this switch relates to the resistance craft workers have to the more extensive forms of workplace reorganization involving the use of teams. Since craft workers have more to lose from the weakening of job demarcation lines, a critical feature of many workplace reforms, they are often more resistant than production workers to the introduction of these changes. This problem produces a trade-off for management. The shift to the use of robots directly increases flexibility in the production process, but it also leads to the employment of more skilled workers who are more resistant to the introduction of new forms of labor relations that also would increase production flexibility.

A third factor contributing to increased variability in production and the need for greater flexibility in labor relations systems is the volatility in product demand induced by macroeconomic flux. This flux could be generated by either cyclical macroeconomic volatility in the countries where U.S.-produced cars are sold or abrupt changes in the price of oil. Cyclical volatility in national economies would produce variation in the volume of motor vehicles demanded and thereby add to the need to adjust production volumes and type rapidly (Piore 1982). The difficulties management planners now face in projecting sales volumes are reflected in recent news. In the fall of 1983 there were reports that although sales levels had risen sharply in the United States, planners remained unsure how much inventory to hold in the light of the uncertainty surrounding sales forecasts (*Business Week*, 1983b).

Uncertainties and volatility in the price of oil can contribute to cyclical volatility in industrial economies and more directly create volatility in consumer preferences and car sales levels. As the U.S. industry learned in the 1970s, changes in oil prices not only sharply alter sales volumes but also modify the mix of sales. Recent news stories provide an illustration of the consequences of the increase in market volatility in their descriptions of the plight of management planners who were puzzled as to whether to build more large cars or more small cars or shift to the production of more sporty cars (*Business Week*, 1983a).

As figures 2.1 and 2.2 illustrated, the 1970s brought heightened volatility in employment and auto production. The relevant issue is whether the trend will continue in the U.S. economy toward greater volatility and frequency in business cycles and other conditions of the

1970s such as abrupt changes in the price of oil. It is difficult to make intelligent forecasts along these lines, yet the likely continuation of the structural problems creating heightened volatility in the 1970s— oil price shocks, government policy responses to the inflation-unemployment trade-off, and the increased exposure of the U.S. economy to world economic events—suggests a continuation in this trend of greater macroeconomic instability.

On balance there are a number reasons why the pressure for more flexibility in labor relations is likely to increase. Furthermore the more U.S. companies move to a specialty product strategy, the greater the use of robotic technology, and the more volatile the macroeconomy, the greater the pressure for increased flexibility in the auto labor relations system.

Cost Pressure
In the face of the slump in auto sales that continued from 1979 until mid-1983 and heightened competition from the Japanese, the U.S. auto industry came under intense pressure to lower costs. Will pressure for cost moderation continue? The sharp rebound in domestic auto sales that started in mid-1983 has led some to predict that the industry has returned to a long-run growth path similar to that of the 1950s and 1960s. Are these predictions accurate? To derive a good forecast of future trends, a number of critical factors that influence future domestic auto sales must be considered: the growth rate of the U.S. and other economies, the competitive pressure generated by foreign producers, and the course of protectionist government policies that might insulate U.S. producers from foreign competition.

A sensible forecast by the M.I.T. International Auto Program predicts annual growth in world demand for motor vehicles of roughly 2 percent through the end of the century (Altshuler et al. 1984).[4] This amounts to a significantly slower growth rate than that which occurred over the postwar years. Yet this projection is far from a doomsday scenario for the industry. With this annual growth in world demand, companies or countries that manage to increase their market share in the world market could grow at a significant pace. And even with this projection of overall growth in world demand, companies and countries that are not competitive in the world market will face severe declines. The same is true even if world demand deviates from the M.I.T. projection. The critical question therefore becomes the state of competitive relations in the world market.

How will U.S. companies fare in the world auto market in the years ahead? Chapter 3 reviewed some of the evidence concerning current cost differentials between U.S. producers and the Japanese companies. If these estimates prove to be accurate, the Big Three would have to succeed in their efforts to narrow the cost differential, or receive the benefits of protectionist relief, or else face sharp increases in Japanese import penetration.

Based on recent trends, there are reasons to believe that protectionism will intervene to ensure at least moderate long-run growth for domestic producers (Altshuler et al. 1984, chap. 10).[5] From the spring of 1981 to the spring of 1984, the U.S. industry has been operating with the protection of a voluntary agreement by the Japanese to limit their imports to 1.68 million cars a year, roughly 22 percent of the domestic market. The Japanese recently agreed to extend these restraints and hold total U.S. exports to 1.85 million vehicles in 1984, which should keep the Japanese share of the U.S. market near 22 percent.

The longevity of the import restrictions, the attractiveness of restrictions to Democratic and Republican administrations alike, and the central role of the auto industry in the U.S. economy suggest that it is unlikely any administration in the near future would let the Japanese share of the U.S. market rise significantly beyond 25 to 30 percent. Furthermore the only situation in which any administration is likely to allow the Japanese share to rise significantly is in an environment where other factors have led to high sales or financial success for U.S.

producers. If Japan's share of the U.S. market is limited below this figure, then one needs a forecast of significant decline in total U.S. auto sales to arrive at a prediction of significant sales declines for domestic producers. This points to the conclusion that on the whole, U.S. producers are unlikely to face sharp long-term declines in sales over the end of the century. This, of course, does not imply that all U.S. companies will have market or financial success nor does it imply the absence of periodic sharp cyclical declines in sales.

The likelihood of at least moderately strong long growth for U.S. producers is enhanced even further if the estimates of a sizable Japanese cost advantage prove to be exaggerated or the U.S. industry is able to improve its competitive standing rapidly. In this case with a 2 percent annual growth in the world market, U.S. producers would face moderate to strong upward long-term growth in motor vehicle sales. At the least, with this growth in the world market and improvement in the U.S. competitive position, the U.S. producers would not be under extreme pressure to lower costs. Of course, even in a scenario of 2 percent annual long-term growth, any sharp cyclical downturns might create more severe immediate financial problems for some producers.

Yet even if U.S. production volumes grow at an annual rate near 2 percent, the situation for auto employment is much less favorable. This follows from the effects that necessary productivity improvements are likely to exert on employment.

Table 6.1 reports employment figures generated assuming the M.I.T. world demand growth predictions, stability in the U.S. share of the world market after 1980, and the assumption of 4 percent annual growth rates in labor productivity.[6] The figures in table 6.1 show a decline of U.S. blue- and white-collar auto industry employment of 20.8 percent from 1979 to 1990 and a further decline of 23.4 percent from 1990 to 2000. The forecast amounts to a drop of 386,000 auto industry employees between 1979 and 2000. These employment pro-

Table 6.1
Employment projections to 2000 (in thousands)

	1979	1990	2000
United States	982.2	778.1	596.4
Europe[a]	2008.9	1591.4	1219.5
Japan	651.3	525.4	463.3
Total	3642.4	2894.9	2279.6

Notes: The employment figures represent blue- and white-collar employment. The following additional assumptions were utilized: 4 percent annual labor productivity growth; Japan's home market grows at 1 percent per year; Japan's market share in the United States and Europe rises from 11.5 percent in 1979 to 13.0 percent in 1980 and beyond; Japan's market share in LDCs rises from 26.6 percent in 1979 to 28.0 percent in 1980 and beyond; no change in the market shares between the U. S. and Europe; a total world output volume of 41.3 million units is assumed for 1979. Production in Japan, the United States, and Europe in 1979 is 32.0 million units (the difference is Communist and LDC production). The 1990 and 2000 employment projections utilize total world car and truck production estimates of 51.2 million units in 1990 and 66.8 million units in 2000.
a. These figures include employment in the following countries: France, Italy, Sweden, the United Kingdom, and West Germany.

jections use the industry definition of SIC 371, the motor vehicles and equipment industry. A broader definition, which includes the total labor input into materials, such as steel, and energy inputs, would yield larger initial employment estimates and larger employment declines.

Alterations in the demand growth, market share, or other assumptions also would change the employment trends; however, it is difficult to derive a scenario that will generate any significant employment growth in the U.S. auto industry if one adopts reasonable assumptions. Furthermore these figures may prove to overestimate employment in the light of all of the potential productivity advances available to the industry. A significant increase in the amount of parts outsourcing from abroad would also bring lower U.S. employment than these projections.

The effects of higher productivity growth rates on these employment projections depend on how widespread are the productivity increases. If the United States were to increase productivity faster than other countries, then the U.S. market share might rise beyond that assumed in this forecast, which would lead to higher sales and employment. Productivity growth rates in all countries greater than the assumed 4 percent figure would have complicated (and hard to predict) effects on U.S. employment since this would lead to greater total world sales as well as lower labor utilization per vehicle.

The employment forecast in table 6.1 suggests that even if U.S. output grows in the long run at a moderately upward rate, the UAW likely will face employment declines that generate pressure for the union to improve workers' job security. Note that the U.S. employment figures in table 6.1 refer to industry but not necessarily UAW-represented employment. If U.S. producers increase their parts sourcing from nonunion domestic suppliers, then the UAW would face even larger membership declines and additional pressure.

In summary, the economic environment is likely to provide continued pressure on labor and management in the U.S. auto industry to moderate costs. Although cyclical slumps and particular competitive problems may lead to extreme pressure for some firms, most U.S. firms probably will face moderate to strong pressure for cost reduction but pressure that is not as extreme as the recent sales slump.

Japanese-Owned Plants in the United States

Honda now produces Accords at a plant in Marysville, Ohio; Nissan produces small trucks in Smyrna, Tennessee (and recently announced plans to produce small cars in the plant); Toyota and GM manufacture jointly a small car in GM's former Fremont assembly plant; and Mazda plans to build cars in Flat Rock, Michigan. These and other Japanese-owned auto plants operating in the United States may function as another environmental pressure that induces change in the labor relations conduct of the Big Three and the UAW.

It appears that in these plants the Japanese companies are trying to import some of the features of their labor relations system or at least introduce an Americanized version of that system (Freedman 1982b). The Honda and Nissan plants so far have operated on a nonunion basis.[7] Both plants utilize very few job classifications and a team style of work organization similar to the GM operating team system. Workers are organized into work teams and have responsibility for inspection, materials handling, and housekeeping duties along with their regular production job responsibilities. In addition, apparently there are pay incentives for workers to learn a variety of production job tasks analogous to GM's pay-for-knowledge system. If these plants are able to operate successfully with nontraditional labor relations systems, they will add to the pressure on the UAW to agree to similar or at least competitive practices in the Big Three.[8]

Pressure on the UAW to agree to nontraditional labor relations practices may follow from the union's efforts to organize the Japanese-owned facilities. The UAW's willingness to accept nontraditional work rule systems in the joint GM-Toyota plant illustrate how this might work. The UAW negotiated with GM and Toyota regarding whether the new plant will recall workers who were laid off from the former GM-Fremont plant and whether those recalls would strictly follow the seniority provisions of the local agreement in the former plant. The negotiations also centered around the union status of the plant and whether the UAW would be automatically recognized.

The agreement reached between GM, Toyota, and the UAW resolved these issues. GM and Toyota agreed to recognize the UAW and to recall a significant number of the former Fremont workers but did not agree to follow strictly the former seniority rights in the rehiring process (Buss and Koten 1983). The UAW agreed to allow a greatly reduced number of classifications in the plant and other work rule changes. The exact terms of the work rules in the plant will not be final until a first contractural agreement is negotiated after the full start-up of production, now scheduled for early 1985. Yet it seems likely that the plant will use nontraditional labor relations practices and thereby add to the pressure on the UAW to agree to similar changes in Big Three plants.

Alternative Future Paths of Labor Relations

How will environmental economic pressures influence the future course of U.S. auto labor relations? The fact that labor relations practices tend to evolve into a well-connected system implies that labor and management do not face a large number of alternative labor relations options, each only slightly different from some other option. As the history of auto collective bargaining shows, the basic operation of a labor relations system resists fundamental change and encourages incremental change only so long as such change does not call into question any of the key terms of the system. In addition the logic of the operation of a labor relations system requires that the various features of any new system fit together well with each other. For example, pay procedures will not persist if they are not well tailored to the structure of bargaining or do not mesh with the defined terms of worker participation in decision making. Therefore labor and management will be choosing from a limited number of alternative paths, each of which entails a set of pay, bargaining structure, and worker involvement procedures. The three paths outlined next appear to be the alternative available to labor and management in the U.S. auto industry.

Status Quo Path

One potential path is continuation of the traditional labor relations system. Wages would continue to be set by formula mechanisms; the connective bargaining structure would maintain standardization in pay and work rules across companies, plants, and work groups and maintain the strong position of the national union; and a job control focus would continue the heavy reliance on formal, written, and arms-length procedures.

The more favorable the environmental economic conditions, the more likely this path and the retention of the traditional labor relations system. Given the strength and stability of the traditional system, even moderate economic growth would most likely lead to retention of the old system. History suggests that unless there is strong pressure to do otherwise, the parties and the features of the traditional labor relations system exert strong pressure for the systems continuation. Both labor and management are attracted to the stability and continuity provided in the traditional system. Furthermore the interconnections that exist across the key features of bargaining strongly reinforce continuation of the current system. The use of wage formulas removes compensation from local bargaining and thereby eliminates trades at the local level involving work rules and wages. This reinforces the tendencies within the connective bargaining structure for standardization and centralization. Meanwhile the wage rules and connective bargaining structure limit the scope of labor-management interactions and leave little room for more extensive worker involvement in decision making, reinforcing the already strong pressures for the maintenance of job control unionism.

The continuation of the traditional labor relations system might include QWL-type programs possessing a limited focus as a supplement to the traditional key features. These programs could be used as a vehicle to address housekeeping issues, provide a forum for increased worker-supervisor communication, and include quality programs or some other mechanism for workers to make suggestions concerning production problems. The QWL programs would then look very much like the programs underway in GM in the early and mid-1970s and would not confront the more serious issues raised by more extensive forms of work reorganization and work rule change.

Some compensation concessions and work rule modifications also might emerge in this path, most likely during cyclical downturns; however, the parties are likely to introduce such concessions only by diverting formula wage increases or possibly by postponing certain scheduled formula increases, or they might make minor adjustments in one or more fringe benefits. It would take more extreme economic pressure to induce labor and management to abandon the wage formulas or particular fringe benefit items, changes that would take the parties down a different labor relations path.

But suppose economic conditions are not even moderately favorable. In this case two radically divergent paths emerge as possibilities. One would involve significant conflict; the other would involve labor-management cooperation and innovative shop floor labor relations.

Conflict Path

In the face of severe pressure to reduce costs in order to improve sale and competitive world standing, it is possible that management in the industry would try to break the UAW and operate on a nonunion basis.[9] In effect U.S. auto management would have to decide to imitate other industries in the United States that have been able to operate fully nonunion or significantly increase the degree to which they operate on a nonunion basis. The high-technology and much of the drug and chemical industries are examples of industries that have been able to stay largely nonunion.[10] Industries that traditionally were either completely or almost fully unionized in the past but now have a significant amount of nonunion participation include the coal, tire, steel, meatpacking, and auto parts industries (Kochan, McKersie, and Cappelli 1984).

Clearly the UAW would aggressively fight any efforts to operate the Big Three companies on a nonunion basis. Consequently this strategy would lead to intense strikes and other forms of conflict. Management is more likely to succeed in this strategy if other conditions such as a weak labor market or a conservative political environment weaken the union's opposition.

GM's experience in its southern plants suggests that a movement to nonunion operation in one part of the Big Three eventually would bring into play labor relations in the rest of that company and maybe in the rest of the industry. In a fight over union status, the UAW is likely to apply pressure in unionized facilities in order to unionize or limit any nonunion facilities. In addition workers are unlikely to be willing to agree to a more open and flexible labor relations system in organized plants when they fear that this might be part of a strategy to remove the union. Events at GM's southern plants in the late 1970s illustrate this point. Therefore auto management in the long run will not be able to pursue simultaneously a nonunion strategy in one part of the company and a cooperative strategy in another part. Consequently to the extent that cooperative programs are successful at improving economic performance, this raises the cost to management of pursuing a nonunion strategy.

The severe economic pressures on the Big Three that would make a nonunion option attractive also would make it unlikely that the companies would open any new plants. So if the auto companies want to pursue the nonunion option, they would have to try to operate some of their existing plants on a nonunion basis. This strategy would be limited by the fact that as of 1980, all of the Big Three plants were organized, and the UAW has union security clauses in all of its national agreements with the Big Three. Therefore this option likely will not be available when the companies would be most interested in it. Overall these factors would make it very costly, if not impossible, for the auto companies to pursue a nonunion strategy.

If a conflict path were to emerge, it is more likely that labor and management would drift into a conflictual relationship rather than initiate it through direct actions by the companies to operate on a nonunion basis. A conflictual path is most likely to emerge if pressures to reduce costs lead management to bargain hard for further pay and work rule concessions and make substantially greater use of outsourcing. Through increased outsourcing, the Big Three could increase their purchase of parts and services produced by lower-cost and nonunion domestic and foreign suppliers. With a gradual but significant increase in outsourcing, UAW-represented auto employment would shrink.[11]

Conflict ensues on this path if the UAW responds to increased outsourcing by initiating strikes or similar actions or if repeatedly frustrated by earlier pay concessions, at some point workers and the UAW leadership refuse further pay and work concessions and initiate militant strike and shop floor actions as part of their resistance to management's demands.

The conflict scenario would entail a breakdown of the traditional system and the reemergence of the kind of prolonged conflict and instability characterizing the union's organizing drives in the 1930s and immediate postwar auto bargaining. It is possible that, unlike in the late 1940s, this conflict would not lead rapidly to stabilized labor relations but rather to prolonged strikes or the transformation of the UAW into a radical union. A critical factor would be the form of any governmental intervention applied to resolve the conflict. It is difficult to predict the form and timing of the return to any more stable pattern of labor relations that might follow this conflict phase; however, the enormous costs this conflict would impose on both management and labor make the emergence of this path likely only if the industry were to face a sustained sales decline and extreme pressure to lower costs.

Cooperative Path
A third potential path is the introduction of greater flexibility into pay and work rules and increased worker involvement in decision making. This path is more likely if the industry were under some pressure to reduce costs and introduce greater flexibility. Moderate economic pressure might induce labor and management to extend recent movements toward an alternative to the existing system. A cooperative path is less likely in the face of extreme economic pressure because the parties would probably pursue more radical alternatives in response to extreme pressure, with management attempting to increase

greatly outsourcing or the union resisting extensive concessions or outsourcing.[12]

Flexibility in Pay Determination
A cooperative path would include many reforms, including more flexible wage determination. Autoworker wages could be made more responsive to macroeconomic conditions and simultaneously allowed to vary more significantly across companies through an expansion in the use of profit sharing or some other form of contingent compensation.[13] This could be accomplished by way of an increase in the profit-sharing plans in place in the GM and Ford 1982–1984 national contracts with the UAW. The expansion of profit sharing might be provided in lieu (fully or partially) of the reintroduction of the 3 percent annual improvement factor formula increase (eliminated in 1982), or profit sharing could partially substitute for full-scale continuation of the traditional COLA escalator. The variation in autoworkers' income provided by an increasing reliance on contingent compensation would shift further away from the cross-company standardization in the traditional connective bargaining structure.

This expansion of profit sharing would be valuable to the industry not because it brought a sustained decrease in compensation but rather because it would provide a better link between the economic conditions in the industry and pay.[14] The use of profit sharing would bring moderation in pay growth or maybe even pay declines during economic downturns in the industry, but it might also produce larger pay increases than would have been generated by traditional formula mechanisms during sales and profit booms.

Another advantage of profit sharing or some other contingent form of compensation is that it would more closely tie workers' interests to the economic performance and success of the firm. Profit sharing would serve to reduce the distinction between workers and managers and in this way combine with increased worker participation in business decisions to improve worker-manager relations. One result might well be a significant productivity increase.

U.S. labor and management could look to the Japanese auto industry for examples of how wages could be linked more closely to economic performance. Autoworkers in the major Japanese auto assembly companies receive an annual bonus roughly equal to one-third of total annual pay (Koshiro 1982, table 10). The size of this bonus is set in company-level negotiations. Potentially the bonus provides a mechanism for autoworkers' pay to vary significantly across companies as a function of each company's financial performance and across time, although in recent years, possibly as a function of the common sustained growth in the Japanese industry and the high degree of interfirm competition, the bonus system apparently has not led to wide pay variation across the major auto firms (Koshiro 1982, p. 197).[15]

Another way the responsiveness of wages to macroeconomic conditions could be increased is through the negotiation of national contracts of shorter duration, say two- or one-year agreements rather than the traditional three-year agreement. The more frequent negotiation of pay increases would allow labor and management to adjust their settlements more closely in alignment with the now more uncertain and changing auto market and inevitably would lead away from the traditional wage formula mechanisms. There has already been some movement in this direction in recent years as the parties shifted away from the traditional form of three-year agreements.[16] Chrysler and the UAW signed a one-year agreement in 1982 and then negotiated a two-year agreement in 1983. The GM and Ford national agreements with the UAW reached in March 1982 were thirty months in length.

Foreign practices could serve as a model. Virtually all foreign auto industries negotiate pay rates through agreements that are of shorter duration than the traditional three-year agreements in the United

States. For example, in Japan, West Germany, and many other European countries, autoworkers' pay increases are set in annual pay negotiations.

In other countries the bargaining structure of wage negotiations often forces a more direct link between negotiations in the auto industry and negotiations in other industries than is the practice in the United States. In the U.S. bargaining structure, the UAW negotiates autoworkers' wages separately from negotiations in other industries. In this structure wage developments in other industries influence settlement terms in the auto industry only very indirectly by setting patterns that affect the expectations of workers and managers.

In Japan, in contrast, each spring (the so-called spring offensive) a pattern-setting wage agreement is negotiated in one of eight large corporations, consisting of Toyota, Nissan, and six other companies in the iron and steel, shipbuilding, and electrical machinery industries (Koshiro 1982, p. 197). This process involves a high degree of discussion within the ranks of the leading unions regarding an appropriate annual wage target and the choice of the target company. Company-level bargaining in the Japanese auto industry typically closely follows the pattern set in the spring. Consequently wage levels are fairly standardized across auto companies, though potentially the bargaining structure permits for the negotiation of differing company wage increases (Galenson 1976, pp. 644–645).

In the West German auto industry wage increases are set in annual regional agreements negotiated by the metalworkers' union (IG Metall) and employer associations.[17] These agreements are supplemented by other multiyear skeleton agreements that cover work conditions, payment systems, and trade union rights. In this process the bargaining goals for the auto industry are set in the context of a debate within the metalworkers' union regarding their wage policies for the wide range of metalworking industries. A second round of company-level bargaining over wages sometimes occurs. This typically involves the negotiation of 1 or 2 percent of additional pay increases in particularly successful companies. In the auto industry this system of regional and supplementary pay bargaining has produced a modest degree of pay divergence across companies. For example, pay rates at Volkswagen in 1975 were approximately 5 percent above the hourly rate in other auto companies (Streeck 1984).

The debate that occurs within the metalworkers' union in West Germany functions somewhat like the spring offensive in Japan by creating a mechanism linking wage developments in the auto industry to wage developments in other major industries. There is evidence that the net effect of these national differences in bargaining structure is to create greater interindustry wage standardization in foreign countries as compared to the United States. Table 6.2 compares average hourly earnings received by workers in other industries in the major auto-producing countries. The figures show that autoworkers have a relatively higher standing in the U.S. earnings distribution as compared to autoworkers in all other countries.[18] By having their wages set

Table 6.2
Ratio of average hourly earnings in motor vehicle industry versus average hourly earnings in all private industry for production workers, 1970 and 1980

	1970	1980
United States	1.31	1.55
West Germany	1.20	1.21
France	1.25	1.16
Italy	1.32	1.01
United Kingdom	1.34	1.09
Japan[a]	1.13	1.23
Sweden	1.19	1.05

Source: Data for France, West Germany, Italy, and the United Kingdom come from Eurostat's harmonized series of hourly earnings. The author is grateful to David Marsden for assisting in the interpretation of these data. U.S. data are from U.S. Department of Labor (various years).
a. These data compare average earnings of production workers in the automobile industry to earnings in all manufacturing industries (not all private industry). The author is grateful to Kazutoshi Koshiro for assisting in their interpretation.

strictly through wage formulas, U.S. autoworkers were able to shield themselves from effects that inflation and recession exerted on the pay of other U.S. workers in the 1970s.

The changes in bargaining structure that would bring autoworkers' pay negotiations in the United States closer to the style of foreign negotiations are enormous and fly in the face of long-standing traditions and organizational loyalties. Consequently although changes along these lines might provide a helpful increase in the link between wage determination and the auto industry's economic conditions, they are unlikely. If wage flexibility were to come to the U.S. auto industry, it would more likely arrive through expansion in profit sharing or through the negotiation of shorter pay agreements.

Work Rule Flexibility
In the U.S. auto industry greater flexibility in the production process and cost reduction also could be developed through a movement away from the traditional job control orientation of labor-management relations. One way to increase flexibility is to broaden job responsibilities and training, which would simplify adjustments in production volume and type. GM's operating team system may well provide a model of how job broadening could be expanded in the U.S. auto industry. The operating team system has a single job classification for production workers and a greatly reduced number of classifications for craft workers. The system uses a pay-for-knowledge system to provide incentives for workers to learn a wider variety of job tasks. In addition team meetings serve as a forum for the discussion of shop floor production and personnel problems.

The operating team system is particularly interesting because it includes some of the procedures that provide the Japanese auto industry with its high degree of flexibility and adaptability. In Japan autoworkers rotate across jobs on a regular basis (Cole 1979). In addition workers regularly receive the training and counseling necessary for the career planning needed to organize this rotation (Inagami 1983).[19] Career planning requires the maintenance of information files listing worker skills and the solicitation of worker views regarding their career objectives through surveys and worker-supervisor discussions, all of which occur in the Japanese auto industry.[20] Job rotation and career planning are important because they serve to lessen Japanese autoworkers' identification with any particular job.

The attachment Japanese autoworkers have to a given job and their interest in defending the jurisdiction of a job also is lessened by the fact that wage levels are strongly linked to worker age through the *nenko* pay system (Cole 1979). For instance, looking at the average base earnings of assemblers working in the largest six companies, Koshiro (1982) finds that the pay received by twenty-five-year-old assemblers is 81 percent of the average pay received by thirty-year-old assemblers and 56 percent of the pay received by forty-year-old assemblers.

This is not to say that skill levels or performance play no role in pay determination in Japan's major auto companies. Job grades that vary as a function of work difficulty do exist. Workers attain a higher grade and higher pay on mastering a wider variety of job tasks in their work area (Cole 1979, pp. 173–176). Furthermore workers typically are rated by their supervisors three times a year. These ratings affect both pay within a given job grade and the size of the bonus workers receive at the end of the year. At Honda the annual bonus can vary by as much as 20 percent on the basis of performance ratings.[21]

The extent of pay variation in basic wages is illustrated by Koshiro's (1983, table 8) description of the variation in earnings in a welding department in one of the major Japanese producers. Koshiro reports that basic wages for the twelve welders in this department varied by 40 percent as a function of both job grade and performance ratings within grades.

Yet in total the Japanese pay system as compared to the U.S. system is one in which pay is set much more in accordance with worker attributes and less according to job characteristics. The net effect of the Japanese structure is to weaken worker ties to jobs and worker resistance to modification in the terms of those jobs. Along with broad training and worker rotation, this makes it relatively easier for Japanese auto firm to adjust to changes in demand mix or volume by shifting workers across tasks and work areas.

This is not to say that broader jobs and training are the only features of the Japanese labor relations system that provide flexibility and adaptability. Temporary workers and subcontractors are used as buffers for volume adjustment (Cole 1973, 1979). Yet it is clear that part of the Japanese advantage in flexibility comes by way of the absence of the rigidities inherent in the U.S. job control orientation where workers see their rights and identity closely tied to a narrow set of tasks.

The U.S. auto industry is not the only case where wages and worker rights traditionally have been tied to narrowly defined jobs. Historically West German autoworkers' wages have been closely linked to job attributes, often through formal job analysis; however, the pressure of heightened volatility and uncertainty in the auto market appears to be producing a shift away from this system, which has many similarities to changes underway in the U.S. auto industry.

In 1980 Volkswagen radically revised its pay system. The basic goal of Volkswagen's new pay system, outlined in the Agreement on Wage Differentiation (abbreviated LODI), is to increase the flexibility of work organization and eliminate the continual need to redefine jobs when new technology is introduced.[22] Volkswagen's new pay system is worthy of close analysis because it is so similar to GM's operating team system.

The unit of evaluation in Volkswagen's pay system is no longer a specific job but a cluster of physically and functionally related jobs that form a working unit. All workers in a unit are assigned to the same job grade and receive the same pay rate. The members of a working unit have input into the way job tasks in the unit are divided up, allowing for the development of job rotation and job enlargement. Workers can be temporarily transferred from one working unit to another. If transferred to a higher-paid unit, workers receive the higher pay plus a bonus for being transferred.

Working units are formally described in terms of their skill and task requirements, but the descriptions are much less detailed and standardized than the traditional individual job classifications. Thus the grading of working units is less sensitive to technological and organizational changes. Management and the works councils at Volkswagen informally agreed that the downgrading of a working unit would occur infrequently.

Formal descriptions of and the pay rates assigned to the working units are negotiated between management and the works council. Both sides accept the subjective and, hence, the negotiated basis of the pay grades. If agreements cannot be reached on the working unit descriptions or pay rates, the issue will be resolved through conciliation and arbitration in governmentally operated labor courts.

This system was accepted because both management and labor at Volkswagen were frustrated by the frequent need to renegotiate pay rates in the face of changes in job content brought by either new technology or alterations in product mix. It was also felt that the use of more sophisticated technologies required better coordination across workers, a coordination previously impeded by the existence of distinct job classifications.

These are the same motivations for the use of operating teams in GM. Consequently it is no surprise that GM's operating teams are structured nearly identically to Volkswagen's new working units. Both use team systems to broaden job responsibilities and lessen the connection between pay rates and job definitions.

One important difference between Volkswagen's move to this more flexible work system and U.S. experience with similar changes is that the metalworkers' union in West Germany and the works council at Volkswagen strongly favored the new system. The metalworkers' union has long supported efforts to develop more broadly defined jobs, seeing this as a way to protect employment and promotion opportunities (Streeck and Hoff 1983b, 1:57). In 1973 in a pathbreaking agreement the union won a commitment by employers and works councils to "exhaust all possibilities for job enlargement and enrichment" (Streeck and Hoff 1982, p. 336). In contrast, in the United States although the UAW has accepted the operating system in a few plants, the plan was a management initiative accepted by the union on limited terms. In some plants the local UAW union strongly resisted the use of the new team system, and craft workers generally have strongly resisted the shift to more broadly defined work and pay systems.

Fewer Rules and More Informal Labor Relations
One of the advantages of broader job classifications and team forms of work organization is that they encourage the development of more informal labor relations and reduce the time-consuming rigidities inherent in more formal adjudication of problems. For example, the team meetings in GM's operating team system allow workers and supervisors to discuss production problems and work assignments and avoid the need for the detailed rules concerning such issues in the traditional local contracts. Another potential advantage is that team meetings provide communication between workers and supervisors, which reduces the need to process complaints through the grievance procedure.

Suppose the use of team systems increased in the U.S. auto industry. What would happen to the role of the union? The development of more informal shop floor labor relations in the U.S. auto industry would change but not diminish the role of the local union. The local union would have to be an active monitor and overseer of the activities of the work teams. This would be an essential role to enable the local union to mediate the inevitable tensions that arise between remaining formal bargaining procedures and the actions of individual work groups. The local union would have to set guidelines regarding any procedures regulating the bounds of work group and worker actions. One of the issues confronting the local union would be managing the diversity of pay rates and work conditions that would arise through the new work organization. A model for this role is the steering committee (sometimes called a planning committee) used in some of GM's plants utilizing the operating team system. The steering committee oversees actions taken by the teams and is called in to resolve problems if a team begins to address an issue deemed to be of concern to the rest of the plant. The steering committee thus stands at the interface between worker participation and bargaining processes and is called on to mediate any tensions or conflicts that arise in that interaction.

Broader job definitions and more flexible work rules require that workers become involved in shop floor production decisions. In addition, for workers and supervisors to set job assignments and resolve problems more flexibly and informally, improved communication is required. Furthermore institutionalized procedures that enable workers and their union to mediate the relationship between shop floor personnel issues and other collective bargaining issues are necessary for the effective operation of the new work systems. For all of these reasons it is artificial to draw a distinction between the worker participation aspects of these new work systems and the basic work rules and work organization of the new systems.

Lessons from West Germany
If the team system were to take hold, on the shop floor level the U.S. auto labor relations system would have to acquire some of the attributes of the West German labor relations system. By participating in personnel decisions regarding work allocation, the work teams would assume some of the responsibilities that in the West German system

are influenced by the works council, a system of worker representation mandated by federal West German law. On the whole worker
teams in the United States would function as an avenue of worker
participation and representation that paralleled the local union. In
this way expansion of the use of team systems in the United States
would move the U.S. labor relations system closer to the form of
the West German system where the works council and the union
function as parallel institutions (Streeck 1981, 1984).

Tracing the similarities between a cooperative U.S. path and the West
German system highlights one of the problems facing developments
in the U.S. auto industry. In the West German system the union's
security and representation rights are guaranteed through federal
codetermination legislation. Consequently the metalworkers' union,
which represents German autoworkers, is less fearful that the activities of the works councils or other managerial strategies might lead to
the demise of union representation rights.

No similar guarantee of representation rights exist for unions in the
United States, which contributes to the unions' fears that team or
other new work organization systems might lead to the demise of
union representation. A partial remedy for these fears would be the
preservation of clear authorization and regulation of team systems in
the union's collective bargaining agreements and the active participation of the local union as a monitor of the activities of the work teams.
In this way union involvement in decision making in the United
States would expand as a prerequisite for union and worker acceptance of the informality inherent in the new work system, further
reason why the drawing of a sharp distinction between work rule
changes and worker or union participation programs would make
little sense where extensive work reorganization takes hold.

The fact that the Big Three companies are now completely organized
by the UAW suggests that the UAW may be well positioned to take
the risks associated with a wider use of team systems. If the UAW and

workers feared that the teams might be used as a device to erode union representation rights, then they would be unlikely to favor significant expansion in the use of teams. This suggests an important irony in the history of GM's southern strategy. GM first introduced the operating team system in its southern nonunion plants. These plants thus functioned as a testing ground for labor relations innovation. Yet the fact that the southern strategy was ended may provide a critical element of security to the UAW without which future expansion in the use of the operating team system might be impossible.

Employment Guarantees

Another instrument management could use to facilitate worker and union acceptance of the new work systems is to increase employment security, though not the specific job security of the work force. The potential functions served by greater employment security are many. The cooperative path is most likely to occur in an economic environment in which the auto companies are under some pressure to reduce costs. As revealed in the 1982 pay concessions and the local work rule concessions, concessions are often accompanied by some form of explicit employment guarantee. The introduction of these guarantees appears to arise from workers' need to be convinced that there will be an increase in employment as a consequence of pay or work rule concessions.

The 1982 national agreements at GM and Ford included a plant closing moratorium, introduced a guaranteed income security benefit program, and initiated pilot employment guarantee negotiations at a sample of plants. It is likely that any further pay concessions would include some sort of explicit improvement in workers' employment security.

Additional employment guarantees are also likely to be part of a cooperative reform strategy because the guarantees provide a way to counteract the insecurity introduced by other features of this path.

The cooperative path would involve a movement away from the traditional written and formalistic procedures and expand the use of team or other forms of work organization involving broader job classifications. One of the reasons workers resist the introduction of these more flexible and informal work rules is that they fear these systems will eventually introduce supervisory discretion and favoritism into layoff decisions. Furthermore workers are often fearful that any productivity gains from the new work systems will lead to job displacement. A way to counteract these fears is to introduce greater employment security along with the new work systems.

The experience in other countries provides some useful lessons. One of the successes of both the Japanese and West German auto labor relations systems is the provision of a significant degree of employment security.[23] In Japan maintenance of a lifetime employment principle for regular full-time workers seems to have reduced workers' fears of technological displacement and contributed to workers' acceptance of broad job definitions and training.[24]

Nevertheless a number of problems make the introduction of employment guarantees particularly difficult in the United States. It is unlikely that the sharp cyclical flux that has characterized demand for more vehicles over the postwar years in the United States will disappear in the future. The earlier discussion of future environmental conditions in fact suggests that this flux may well increase. Consequently if employment were to be guaranteed for some group of workers in the U.S. auto industry, employers would have to develop an outlet or mechanism to absorb the flux in labor demand that results from fluctuations in product demand.

In West Germany the migration of guest workers often provides an outlet for production volume flux and allows German automakers to provide significant (though not complete) employment stability for native German workers. In addition the use of short-time work is subsidized by the federal government in West Germany and thereby encourages the use of hours rather than employment variation as a response to volume flux (Sengenberger and Kohler 1982).

In Japan the use of temporary workers and the ability to pass any cyclical adjustment problems to supplier segments in the industry help the major auto producers maintain the lifetime employment principle for permanent workers. The Japanese auto companies also purchase a more significant share of their parts from suppliers than do U.S. auto companies. The absence of employment guarantees within the supplier industry and the scope of parts subcontracting gives the main assembly companies in Japan an outlet for volume flux.[25]

In West Germany and, to an even greater extent, Japan, the existence of more flexible work rules allowing the transfer of workers and the existence of multiskilled workers ease the adjustment to cyclical flux in auto demand. In Japan workers are shifted across work groups and occasionally even across member companies within a corporate trading group to facilitate the continuation of employment guarantees in the major firms (Galenson 1976).[26] The ready transfer of workers requires flexible job definitions, transfer rights, and broad skill acquisition. These are the work rule systems that are lacking in the United States and are the work rules that employment guarantees are supposed to help encourage.

The U.S. industry thereby is caught in a dilemma regarding employment guarantees and more flexible work systems. The employers need more flexible work rules in order to ease the burden of and adjustment to greater employment guarantees. But they need the presence of employment guarantees to help convince workers to agree to these changes. A partial solution would be the simultaneous negotiation of more flexible work rules and enhanced employment security. Yet the actual negotiation of such package deals is not so easy. Some of the difficulties were revealed in the negotiations that occurred in the pilot employment guarantee (PEG) sites at Ford and

GM in the aftermath of the signing of the 1982 national contracts. The 1982 national agreements at Ford and GM provided that 80 percent of the work force in the pilot sites would be guaranteed employment during the duration of the national agreement after the local union and plant management negotiated a revised local agreement. Management subsequently entered these local negotiations with the objective of altering work rules in a manner that would make it easier to transfer workers and in other ways adjust to future production volume flux; however, the negotiations over the new local agreements became bogged down in the experimental sites.[27] Apparently a key source of the failure to negotiate new local agreements implementing the employment guarantees was workers' resistance to management's demands for significant work rule changes. A tentative agreement was reached at one site, Ford's Chicago assembly plant, in the spring of 1983, but the agreement was overwhelmingly rejected by workers. When the local PEG negotiations extended on through 1983, the employment guarantees became largely irrelevant in the light of the industry's recovery. In the end only one plant ever signed a PEG agreement, a Ford parts plant in Rawsonville, Michigan, which signed a PEG agreement in March 1984 (Bureau of National Affairs 1984).

Labor-Management Relations at the Corporate Level

If a cooperative path were to emerge in the U.S. auto labor relations system, changes in corporate labor-management relations also would be required. In a cooperative path, at the national level labor and management would have to develop a more informal relationship in which greater communication regarding business and production decisions was regularly being provided to the union leadership. In part the union's involvement in a broader array of business decisions would likely grow out of the union's desire (or insistence) that it be informed of such decisions before it would be willing to agree to any form of contingent compensation scheme. One of the reasons unions and workers have resisted adoption of profit sharing is their fear that management would manipulate profit sharing to its own ends. Provision of more extensive financial information to the union leadership could lessen those fears.

The emergence of greater corporate-level contacts between labor and management would bring a shift away from the arms-length nature of the traditional job control style of labor relations. Steps already taken in this direction include the corporate-level mutual growth forums; the granting to the vice-presidents of the UAW the right to address the Ford and GM boards of directors semiannually; and the placement of Douglas Fraser on the Chrysler board of directors. An elaboration of a more cooperative path would require an extension of these steps.

One of the important points to note from this development is that it provides another illustration of the interconnected nature of the labor relations system. The argument outlined is that changes in pay setting procedures, the shift toward profit sharing, would lead labor and management toward a more informal and broader range of contacts and away from a job control orientation. In an analogous manner, the introduction of work teams and the expansion of worker participation on the shop floor would lead to modification of another basic feature of the auto labor relations system, the connective bargaining structure.

Work team systems and worker involvement inevitably would lead to diversity in pay and employment conditions across work groups and firms. The standardization that is part of the traditional connective bargaining structure would be lessened, although the UAW might still want to maintain standardization in some employment conditions or limit the range of variation allowed in particular items. The difficult task for the union would be to maintain the desired degree of standardization while at the same time allowing the experimentation and other by-products of increased worker involvement in production decisions. In effect the national and regional union must develop an institutionalized process analogous to the role of the plant-level steering committees, which allow the local union to mediate the relationship between shop floor rules and collective bargaining procedures in GM's operating team plants.

The cooperative path may well include a moderation in the growth rate in autoworkers' and management's compensation as part of cost reduction efforts. In addition the amount of parts outsourcing might also rise as part of management's efforts to lower costs; however, in contrast with managerial efforts in the conflictual strategy, here compensation concessions or outsourcing would not be the mainstay of the cost reduction efforts.

Although this cooperative path might well include greater reliance on contingent compensation that tied pay to company performance, it is not essential that such pay procedures exist for the path to be viable. One determining factor would be the extent to which the financial status of the various producers remained similar. If all of the companies were facing similar economic pressures and were in roughly similar financial situations, there would be less need for pay variation across the companies, although contingent compensation would still be valuable as a way to link pay to variation in the industry's level of performance. The UAW might decide that pay standardization was a useful counterbalance to the diversity in work rules and work organization that would arise in a world of work teams and increased worker involvement.

Some analysts have speculated that the auto industry is likely to follow the example set by American Airlines, since followed by a number of other airlines, and create a two-tiered wage system (Rotbart 1983). In this pay system newly hired workers receive wage rates significantly below the rates received by current employees (32 percent less at American Airlines). I believe that a two-tiered wage system is unlikely to be accepted by the UAW; even if it were adopted, the system probably would contribute little to help the industry lower costs. The UAW is unlikely to accept two-tiered wages because the system would violate the union's long-standing policy of pay standardization, a policy the union fought for strenuously. In any case lower pay rates for new employees would not make much difference if forecasts of severe long-term employment decline for the auto industry are realized. These forecasts imply that there would be few new employees hired.

Given that many of the tactics utilized in the conflict path are inconsistent with the cooperative path, management will confront a clear trade-off as it chooses which path it would like to encourage. If management were to find that cooperative programs were yielding significant payoffs in improved productivity, then more aggressive demands by management for pay concessions, or significant increases in the amount of outsourcing, or a direct nonunion strategy would become less attractive because these steps would jeopardize the cooperative programs. Similarly if management chose a nonunion or heavy outsourcing strategy, there would be little purpose to devote resources to cooperative programs, which in any case would probably show little success in this context.

Corporate Strategies

As history shows, although the economic environment will encourage the movement to one of the three labor relations paths, it will not strictly determine which path is chosen. Labor and management have a degree of strategic choice regarding the course of labor relations. Consequently it is likely that varying company strategies will emerge, with some companies choosing a more cooperative path while others preserve the traditional labor relations system.

The U.S. auto companies responded to the 1973–1983 sales slump with different labor relations strategies. These differences are interesting in their own right and also are useful as an indicator of future strategies.

At one level it is possible to divide the U.S. producers on the basis of whether in response to the sales downturn they made a significant effort to initiate cooperative programs on the shop floor. GM and Ford initiated these programs. At GM these programs were called quality of working life efforts; at Ford the label used for similar programs was employee involvement. The extent to which these programs took hold in GM and Ford plants varied enormously, yet cooperative programs were a key part of the recovery strategies in both companies. In contrast, Chrysler and American Motors did not have similar shop-floor-level cooperative programs. Both Chrysler and American Motors did negotiate pay and work rule concessions with the UAW, and Chrysler did put Douglas Fraser, then president of the UAW, on its board of directors; however, neither company had any program similar to the QWL or EI programs underway at GM and Ford, for a number of reasons. Chrysler and American Motors faced more extreme financial situations than either GM or Ford. Chrysler and AMC management apparently decided that the payoff to cooperative programs was not quick enough or substantial enough to be worthy of the investment needed for the start-up of the programs. Both companies emphasized other programs as the centerpiece of their recovery strategies. Chrysler's strategy used the active salesmanship of its chairman, Lee Iaccoca, and American Motors relied on financing from and a merger with Renault.

Part of the explanation for these divergent strategies also may lie in the personal preferences of the corporate and union leadership. Neither the UAW vice-presidents in charge of the Chrysler and AMC departments nor the corporate management of these companies favored such programs. Ford, on the other hand, had the benefit of Don Ephlin, vice-president of the UAW Ford Department, who actively supported the EI programs. While at GM the momentum created earlier by Irving Bluestone helped carry along the QWL programs. In addition, at GM, Alfred Warren, also a strong supporter of QWL, had become vice-president of labor relations.

There also were differences between the strategies adopted at GM and Ford. There was wider local experimentation in GM. GM introduced the operating team system among all production workers in ten of its plants by the end of 1983, which brought extensive revisions to traditional shop floor labor relations practices. There was no counterpart to these team plants in Ford, although in a number of Ford plants a few departments had adopted single classification systems.

GM first tried out the operating team design in its southern plants and then introduced the system in a few new or refurbished northern plants. Ford, because it faced a larger downturn, was not opening or refurbishing facilities to the same extent as GM and consequently lacked new facilities in which to experiment with the operating team or similar approaches. It also seems that in the early and mid-1970s the organizational development and research group within GM was relatively more aggressive at devising and pushing the use of teams than their counterparts inside Ford.

Although GM developed a wider divergence in local labor relations practices, at the top corporate and union level during the 1979 to 1983 period, there appeared to be a less cooperative relationship at GM compared to Ford. At GM there was a strained relationship concerning QWL programs during this period between the chairman of the company, Roger Smith, and the vice-president of the UAW in charge of GM, Owen Bieber.[28] This strain appeared on the day the 1982 agreement was signed: Smith announced a revised bonus plan for top executives without prenotifying the union leadership. The union and workers reacted angrily, arguing that it was inappropriate for GM to consider improving executive bonuses after workers had agreed to significant pay concessions (*Wall Street Journal* 1982).

In contrast, at Ford, after the 1982 agreement (which was first reached at Ford), Pete Pestillo, the corporate vice-president of labor relations, and Don Ephlin, vice-president of the Ford Department in the UAW, were appearing repeatedly at news conferences, on television shows, and at professional industrial relations meetings and seminars. In these appearances Pestillo and Ephlin went to great lengths to suggest that a new relationship built on mutual trust had been started at Ford.[29] These appearances were largely symbolic, but they did accurately convey that Pestillo and Ephlin had forged a close working relationship. At the same time, the chairman and president of Ford were repeatedly making speeches in which they reaffirmed that a new cooperative relationship between Ford and the UAW was underway.[30] Ephlin's strong support for the EI programs certainly must have been part of the reason why he was so warmly embraced by Ford management. This cooperation also appeared in television advertisements for Ford products, which included pictures of the UAW emblem and statements from workers.

A similar cooperative relationship did not emerge at GM between Roger Smith and Owen Bieber. The fact that Bieber was lukewarm toward the QWL programs and took a position markedly less supportive than his predecessor, Irving Bluestone, clearly was part of the explanation for this development.

A large risk is taken in a strategy that relies heavily on the relationship between corporate management and the top union leadership as a way to redirect labor relations because changes in any of the key individual actors can produce sharp changes in labor-management relations. Ford faced one of these changes in personality and individual philosophy when, after Owen Bieber replaced the retiring Douglas Fraser as UAW president, Ephlin was reassigned to the GM Department, and Stephen Yokich became the new vice-president of the UAW-Ford Department. Yokich had a much less supportive attitude toward cooperative programs than did Ephlin.

One of the critical issues confronting both GM and Ford is finding a way to sustain any cooperative spirit generated with the UAW and workers in the face of their recent increases in outsourcing. Both GM and Ford recently took steps to reduce their long-term production of small cars in the United States. GM plans to import small cars from Isuzu and Suzuki and jointly produce cars that will have a high Japanese content with Toyota in California. Ford announced plans to assemble small cars in Mexico that will be exported to the United States (*Business Week* 1984a). In addition, both companies, along with Chrysler and American Motors, have markedly increased their foreign sourcing of parts (Altshuler et al. 1984).

GM and Ford face the risk that increased outsourcing will antagonize workers and the UAW to the point that cooperative programs are jeopardized. Having placed significant emphasis on cooperative programs and invested substantial energy and money in these programs, GM and Ford have a lot more to lose than Chrysler and American Motors if the reaction of workers and the UAW to increased outsourcing induces a shift to either a more conflictual or status quo labor relations path.

Basic economic trends in the world auto industry are pushing the U.S. auto companies to increased outsourcing. In the face of the large economic advantages of outsourcing, if labor were to force management to eliminate any increase in outsourcing as a precondition for labor's participation in workplace reforms, then the cooperative path would have to yield extremely large gains in productive efficiency for the companies not to be inclined to choose more outsourcing and sacrifice the efforts at cooperation. Furthermore since workers and the UAW are likely to agree to significant work rule and work organization reforms only when there is economic pressure to do so, inevitably some increase in outsourcing will occur simultaneously with any meaningful movement along the cooperative path.

An appropriate policy and scope for outsourcing cannot be decided in isolation from the other changes underway in labor relations. The critical issue for management is to decide if it is going to pursue a basically confrontational stance with labor or cooperatively try to seek an alternative to the existing labor relations system. Once the general path of labor relations is chosen, the task for management is to decide where outsourcing or any other particular issue fits within that broad labor relations path. For instance, management may conclude that it will have to pass up outsourcing opportunities that are cost-effective in the short run in order to provide the employment security necessary as part of a cooperative path.

Union Strategies

The UAW also will make strategic choices that influence the course of future labor relations. One key issue is the extent to which top union leadership supports cooperative programs and any other shift away from the traditional labor relations system. Some evidence regarding viewpoints in the UAW recently was provided in the selection of a replacement for Douglas Fraser, retiring president of the union. There were three leading candidates seeking the presidency of the UAW: Don Ephlin, vice-president of the UAW Ford Department; Owen Bieber, vice-president of the UAW GM Department; and Raymond Majerus, national secretary-treasurer of the UAW. Although there were a number of differences among the three candidates, the sharpest concerned their views toward cooperative programs. Ephlin was a strong supporter of the EI programs at Ford, as he had been of the QWL programs at GM when he served as a regional director under Bluestone prior to being assigned to the Ford Department in 1979. Ephlin made clear his support for the shop floor cooperative programs and his new cooperative relationship with Pestillo. Bieber and Majerus, on the other hand, were lukewarm at best toward QWL programs.

In the winter of 1983, the UAW executive board voted to endorse Bieber to succeed Fraser, an endorsement later ratified in the UAW's annual convention (Bureau of National Affairs 1982d). Although the specific numbers were never made public, apparently a first vote of the executive board led to the withdrawal of Ephlin, and then Bieber won in a head-to-head vote against Majerus (Bureau of National Affairs 1982b). The signal implied by this choice is that a majority of the union's executive board rejected Ephlin's strong support of cooperative programs and endorsed Bieber's less supportive and cautious stance.

At the same time it is clear that there does not exist a militant and radical opposition to the recent policies adopted by the UAW among the executive board of the UAW. A group of local leaders strongly and vocally opposed the concessions agreed to at Ford and GM in the spring in 1982.[31] Yet none of the executive board of the union openly joined this opposition group. All of the executive board of the UAW belong to the Reuther coalition that has dominated the union for the past thirty years.[32] It is possible, of course, that a more radical leadership could emerge, perhaps in response to the pursuit of a nonunion strategy on the part of management or after repeated further pay concessions, actions that would lead to a more conflictual labor-management relationship. But currently there appears to be little support for such militant action among the union's top leadership, making it less likely that a conflictual path will emerge.

Workers' evaluation of the advantages and risks of the various labor relations options clearly is influenced by political views. More radical workers who are suspicious of management's motives tend to oppose the cooperative path on grounds that it opens the door to favoritism, weakens worker security, and ultimately weakens the bargaining power of the union.

Whether workers are in craft or production skill ranks also appears to influence workers' views regarding the various paths. Craft workers generally are inclined to oppose work systems that reduce the number of job classifications, believing that the new work systems weaken craft identity and bargaining power. In addition skilled workers traditionally have a lot of independence and variety on their jobs and see less of a gain from the job enlargement aspects of work reorganizations.

A worker's age also affects assessment of the alternative labor relations paths. The status quo path would preserve the traditional wage formulas and consequently, at least in the short run, produce higher wages than a cooperative path. Higher wages and the absence of the cost savings achieved through work rule changes and work reorganization will lead to lower auto sales and employment levels in the long run. Yet more senior workers, who are protected by seniority layoff and job bidding rights, are less likely to face any layoffs produced as a result of this lower employment. The more senior workers, however, would face any risks or discomforts produced by the work rule changes that were part of the alternative cooperative path. The team system also appears to be less attractive to more senior workers because it reduces the role of seniority in the allocation of jobs. Consequently the status quo path is a safer path and one particularly attractive to high seniority workers.

The 1984 National Contract Negotiations

The negotiation of new national contracts covering UAW workers at GM and Ford in the fall of 1984 provided a further indication of emerging corporate and union strategies. These negotiations occurred in an economic environment that shifted bargaining power to labors' advantage. From early 1983 on, auto sales and profits were buoyed by a strong macroeconomic recovery and the advantages provided by the continuation of voluntary import restrictions on Japanese cars. In 1983, GM and Ford respectively posted profits of $3.7 billion and $1.9 billion, and earnings in the first half of 1984 of $3.2 billion and $1.8 billion. These profits were in part generated by the shift in consumer demand to larger cars and full option models. By mid 1984, constrained by previous plant closings, Ford and GM assembly plants were running at or near full capacity, particularly for the production of large cars.

The union's bargaining stance also was strengthened by workers' angry response to the substantial bonuses awarded executives at Ford and GM as part of their 1983 compensation packages. For example, Philip Caldwell, chairman of Ford, received a combined salary and bonus in 1983 of $1.4 million and earned $5.9 million through the appreciation of stock purchased in his long-term compensation package (*Business Week* 1984d). Roger Smith, chairman of GM, was awarded $1.5 million in salary and bonuses. Many interpreted these bonuses as a signal that auto management believed the industry had fully recovered from its problems. One group of autoworkers (the coalition in favor of restore and more) called for a 1984 contract settlement providing substantially more than a restoration of 1982 contract concessions.

GM was eventually designated as the UAW's target company and when negotiators were unable to reach a settlement by the September 14 deadline, a strike was called. The UAW struck only seventeen plants, although the targeted plants were those assembling relatively high priced cars. Six days later the strike was ended with the announcement of a tentative contract of three years' duration.

The new settlement provides first-year wage increases of 1 percent to assembly workers and up to 3.5 percent increases to certain skilled trades, and average increases of 2.25 percent. In the second and third year of the agreement workers receive lump sum payments amounting to 2.25 percent of their annual wages.[33] In contrast to the first-year increases, these lump sum payments will not be included in the base wages used to determine pensions, overtime, and other benefits. Each worker also will receive $180 upon ratification of the settlement, and the profit-sharing program initiated in the 1982 national contract is continued. It is estimated that in 1984 GM workers will receive approximately $1,000 from the profit-sharing program. The wage settlement also continued the COLA formula, although 24 cents of COLA-generated increases were diverted to cover the cost of rising fringe benefits.

This wage package represents a compromise between the union's desire for full restoration of the traditional wage formulas and the company's desire to provide lower increases and a more direct link between future wage increases and company performance. On the one hand the settlement restores the COLA formula intact. The traditional annual improvement factor, however, was eliminated. The scheduled 2.25 per cent average annual increases are somewhat lower than the traditional 3 percent AIF, vary in size by job classification, and also modify the traditional pattern by not building all of these increases into base rates. In effect, the parties substituted profit sharing and lump sum increases for the traditional AIF formula wage increase. The retention of profit sharing also ensures that autoworkers' annual incomes will vary across the Big Three somewhat as a function of company performance, although the magnitude of this variation will be small.[34]

The most innovative part of the 1984 settlement is a new job security program covering current workers who in the future are displaced from their jobs due to either technological advances, corporate reorganizations, outsourcing, or other negotiated productivity improvements. Under the new job security program workers displaced for any of these reasons will be placed into a reserve pool (bank) and receive full pay while waiting to be transferred or retrained for jobs elsewhere in GM. The program will draw on a $1 billion fund and will last for six years, which is three years beyond the duration of other features of the contract. This job security program will not cover workers laid off because of sales volume reductions, and a labor-management committee will have the difficult task of ruling whether any given layoff is covered by the program or is due to sales declines.

The new job security program compensates workers displaced by technological change or outsourcing and thereby creates a financial discentive for the company to initiate actions that create such displacement. But the program does not explicitly limit management's rights to outsource or introduce new technology, which continues the union's longstanding acceptance of technological change. Nor does the new program commit management to any specific future employment levels. The design of the job security program is similar to that of the supplementary unemployment benefits program by compensating workers, creating financial penalties for layoffs and relying on fund financing.

The cost and coverage of the job security program are fairly modest. The billion dollar job security fund can provide expenditures of roughly $475 per GM worker per year or full income and fringe benefit support ($50,000) to roughly 4,000 workers per year. Furthermore, in the face of ongoing technological change, GM in any case very likely would have had to spend money training workers to handle this new technology. Consequently, some of the expenditures from the new job security program may only substitute for other training expenses. Yet like other fringe benefit programs the UAW has negotiated, the new job security program may expand in scope and resources over time.[35]

The new job security program also may prove to be a valuable supplement to labor and management's cooperative efforts. Workers often fear participation programs or technological change on the grounds that resulting productivity improvements will jeopardize their job security. More flexible and informal work rules and work organization are feared because they create the possibility that supervisors will exploit workers once traditional contractual rules are reduced in scope. The enhancement of workers' job security and the creation of a more explicit career link between auto workers and their employers may lessen these fears.

The establishment of labor-management committees to decide whether or not workers have been displaced as a result of productivity improvements or outsourcing versus demand factors might have significant long-run implications for the industry's connective bargaining structure. Through the committees, national union representatives may become more involved in plant-level issues. Outsourcing decisions frequently are made only after the failure of efforts by plant management to lower in-house production costs through work rule or other changes. When a joint job security committee is called in to decide the cause of a layoff it might be drawn into a debate over which work rules the local union is willing to modify in an effort to keep business in-house and avoid outsourcing in the first place. There are now a number of labor-management committees operating at the plant level, including the joint councils for enhancing job security and the competitive edge (mutual growth forums) and the joint training committees initiated in the 1982–1984 national contracts. It remains to be seen how much interaction occurs across these various committees and the degree to which any such interaction leads to a linking of various issues or to increased national union involvement in plant and local union affairs.

The new job security program builds on the guaranteed income stream program and the training and development program introduced in the 1982–1984 contracts at Ford and GM, and on the SUB program. The combination of all these programs provide a high degree of income security to autoworkers. These programs, however, do not protect auto workers from declines in employment that will follow if the Big Three lose even more of their share of the domestic auto market. The critical determinant of future employment levels is the degree to which the 1984 settlement and other ongoing measures improve the competitive standing of the Big Three.

Some positive effects on industry competitiveness will result from the fact that the 1984 GM-UAW settlement avoided a major strike and seemed to cast a positive tone on labor-management relations. At the same time the wage increases provided in the 1984–1987 settlement are unlikely to narrow the gap between U.S. wage rates and those abroad. Furthermore, the structure of the pay increases included in the 1984 contract provides only small movement toward the creation of direct links between pay and company performance. Consequently, improvement in the competitive standing of the Big Three will depend heavily on the extent to which work rule changes and new forms of work organization are adopted at the plant level which both lower costs and increase the flexibility of the production process. Constrained by the existing bargaining structure which separates the national negotiation of pay from the local negotiation of work rules, however, the 1984 settlement provides no assurance of future work rule change. Are the Big Three likely to succeed in making the kind of work rule changes that are needed to improve their competitive standing? There are a number of key plants that shortly will provide indications of the likely future scope and success of work rule and work organization changes.

At GM, the extent of work rule and work organization change will be influenced strongly by how local contract negotiations are resolved at two new assembly plants. Since 1983 the Lake Orion (Pontiac, Michigan) and Wentzville (St. Louis) assembly plants have been operating with a team system which includes a single job classification for production workers and a pay-for-knowledge system. Under the terms of the GM-UAW national agreement management has the right to set a new plant's first work rules, but then must negotiate a local contract with the local UAW bargaining unit once the new plant attains full-scale production. In the fall of 1984 the Lake Orion and Wentzville plants began to negotiate their first local agreements, and at both plants the local union was expressing a high degree of resistance to the team and pay-for-knowledge systems. These plants are critical because they test GM's ability to spread the use of team systems, heretofore primarily used in parts plants, to assembly plants which traditionally have had more difficult labor-management relations and where the threat of job loss to outsourcing is less severe.

Additional indications of the likely future scope of work rule and work organization reform will come from those plants where QWL

programs have expanded to the point that they address basic productivity concerns. There evidence will surface regarding whether labor
and management have been able to develop mechanisms linking
worker participation and collective bargaining processes.

GM's decision regarding the future production of small cars in the
United States also will be made shortly and have significant impacts
on the course of labor relations reforms. In 1983, GM created the
Saturn project to debate and potentially plan the production of a
small car in the United States. GM's intent was to use the Saturn
project as a mechanism to redesign production and labor relations so
as to enable cost competitive domestic production of a small car. The
Saturn project is noteworthy because it involves union and worker
representatives in the planning stage of technology and car design.
Workers and union representatives participating in the project have
visited Japanese, team, and non-union plants in the United States in
an effort to learn about new forms of labor relations and work organization. As part of the 1984–1987 GM-UAW contract, GM stated an
intent to keep the Saturn project in the United States. Although ex-
actly what kind of car and labor relations practices are included in the
eventual Saturn production set-up remain to be decided.[36]

Like the new assembly plants, the Saturn project illustrates that the
most far-reaching innovations in labor relations are being introduced
in cases where new business is at stake. This represents the same
pattern revealed in the course of local work rule bargaining during
the 1979 to 1983 sales downturn: workers' willingness to adjust work
rules more readily where these changes explicitly guarantee greater
employment. The Big Three continue to face many difficulties in introducing labor relations innovations in such sites. Yet even if they
are able to do so, labor and management still will face the even more
difficult task of spreading innovative labor relations practices to
existing plants where the connection between labor relations and
employment security is less explicit.

Summary

The future course of auto labor relations will be affected by economic developments in the world auto industry. At this point it appears that the economic environment will produce moderate pressure for cost reduction, thus encouraging the parties to choose either a status quo or a cooperative path. If economic pressures turn extreme, then it is more likely that extensive outsourcing or a nonunion strategy would be chosen, either of which is likely to induce significant labor-management conflict. Even in the face of the pressures exerted by environmental factors, it should be remembered that the history of auto bargaining shows that labor and management retain a significant degree of choice regarding the direction of labor relations.

The temptation to respond to the current upturn by allowing the old labor relations system to reassert itself is powerful. Retention of the traditional system with minor modifications may well be an easier and safer path. The logic of labor relations, however, limits the potential gains from incremental modification of the traditional system. Productive changes made to any one of the systems features inevitably would require significant change in some other feature of the system. Furthermore, the status quo path would not adequately respond to intensified international competition and the ongoing structural changes underway in the world auto market and in production technologies. In particular, minor modification of the existing system would not provide the flexibility required in production methods as a result of uncertain markets and specialty product strategies.

Alternatively, a cooperative path could be encouraged through the adoption of a package of measures including wage growth moderation, enhanced employment security, work rule flexibility and team forms of work organization, and increased union and worker participation in business and strategic decisions.

Wage growth moderation could be introduced if the parties would move even farther away from the use of wage formulas. Wage moderation could be linked to a shift to more contingent compensation if the rate of growth in compensation were tied explicitly to corporate economic performance through an expansion of profit sharing. Greater use of contingent compensation would have the virtue of automatically increasing the future responsiveness of employment conditions to environmental economic pressures while also increasing workers' identifications with the long-run health of the firm.

Enhanced employment security could be provided by extending the guaranteed income stream concept down to workers with lower seniority, expanding the job security program introduced in 1984, and meshing these programs with the supplementary unemployment benefit program so as to provide a secure lifetime career to autoworkers. This sort of career security would link workers' interests more closely to the firm while reducing fears of technological displacement or insecurities induced through the movement to more informal and flexible systems of work organization. To make the career employment concept succeed, training, human resource planning, and career planning on a scale much beyond current efforts would be required.

In turn, the expansion of team systems and other work rule changes on the shop floor could lower costs by providing greater flexibility in human resource allocation and reducing the reliance on written procedures. As discussed earlier, an essential ingredient for the success of a more flexible and informal system of work organization is greater worker participation in business and strategic decisions at plant and corporate levels. On the shop floor such participation would be necessary to replace the security previously provided to workers by the heavy reliance on detailed rule making. Increased union involvement in decision making at the corporate level would serve a related function while also facilitating the national union's role in any extended job security or contingent compensation programs.

Now is an opportune time for labor and management to take the steps necessary to develop a new labor relations system. The steps outlined above would in many ways build on some of the contractual changes adopted in the 1982 GM and Ford agreements and the 1984 settlement, and on other more informal changes that have been occurring in the industry's labor relations conduct. Where these steps would differ from recent events is in their effort to reorient labor relations holistically to the point of creating an integrated new system.

Recent events do not reveal consistent movement along one path or another. On the one hand there are some signs of extensive innovation in shop floor labor relations, particularly in GM's operating team plants. At the same time, the inclination to retain the traditional system and follow the status quo path appears to be strong, a desire most clearly illustrated by the union's efforts to retain formula wage increases and maintain a separation between worker participation programs and collective bargaining processes and by management's self-serving compensation policies.

The interconnections and logic of labor relations limit the range of choices available as future options. In the light of those limits, whether they choose the cooperative path or not, labor and management need to develop a clear vision of the path they want and consistent policies to move auto labor relations along it.

| 7 | The Relationship between Labor Relations in the Auto and Other U.S. Industries |

U.S. industries such as steel, trucking, airlines, meatpacking, rubber, and communications over the last few years have faced intensified international competition, competition from low-cost nonunion domestic plants, and in some cases the effects of deregulation. In response to these economic pressures, many of these heavily unionized industries were changing their labor relations practices in a manner similar to the changes introduced in auto collective bargaining. As in auto, labor and management in these industries were searching for ways to introduce greater flexibility in pay and work rule procedures and lower labor costs.

Commonalities in labor relations changes were induced in part because of the similarities in the environmental pressures both auto and other unionized industries were facing. Another reason why there were so many similarities in the modifications made to labor relations practices was that many industries traditionally relied on a labor relations system similar to that in the auto industry.

To the extent that other unionized industries recently have responded to economic pressures by copying bargaining innovations first introduced in the auto industry, this preserved the traditional role the auto industry has played as an innovator and pattern setter in U.S. labor relations. Yet as other industries made more and more extensive changes to their labor relations practices, the possibility emerged that changes initiated in other unionized industries eventually will surpass those in auto and in the process operate as another environmental pressure inducing change in the auto industry. Given these complex interactions, it is worthwhile to look closely at recent labor relations developments in unionized industries in the United States other than auto.

Rise of a Nonunion Alternative to Collective Bargaining

In the auto industry the pressure for cost reduction comes primarily from an increase in foreign competition. Other unionized industries also have felt the brunt of heightened international competition; in addition competitive pressure followed from the effects of deregulation in industries such as trucking, communication, and airlines. Furthermore in these and other industries, the rise of nonunion competition posed a significant new competitive challenge. Industries where nonunion firms have expanded sizably in recent years include the construction, trucking, steel, rubber, meatpacking, and airlines industries.

In some of these industries nonunion competition arose from the entry of nonunion firms. For example, in the steel industry, minimills (nearly all of which were nonunion) grew to 25 percent of the industry (Salpukas 1984). In trucking, owner operators (again nearly all nonunion) expanded their share of the industry in the face of the entry permitted by trucking deregulation. In the airlines industry the importance of nonunion carriers such as Delta, People Express, and New York Air expanded enormously.

In a number of other industries nonunion competition emerged by way of the growth of subsidiaries or plants operating on a nonunion basis within formerly completely unionized companies. Many construction, rubber, and trucking companies fit this pattern (Kochan, McKersie, and Cappelli 1984).

In part the competitive pressure generated by nonunion plants arises from the fact that they pay lower wages than union plants. For example, the pay scales in the nonunion steel minimills are roughly $5 per hour below union rates (*Business Week* 1984b). Nonunion airline carriers often pay pilots salaries significantly below those in the major union carriers; moreover nonunion pilots work more hours.

Lower wages are not the only competitive advantage held by the nonunion firms. A particularly troublesome problem is created for union firms by the fact that many of the nonunion firms operate with work rules and work organization systems that are less costly than those in unionized firms. Many of the growing nonunion plants utilize work team systems, pay for knowledge, and more direct communication between workers and supervisors (Verma 1983; Klein 1983; Foulkes 1980). There is accumulating evidence that these nonunion work systems are significantly more efficient than the traditional work practices utilized in unionized plants based on narrow job classifications and detailed regulation of work practices through highly formalized rules (Verma 1983; Kochan, McKersie, and Cappelli 1984). The nonunion work systems have developed to the point that they now represent a sophisticated alternative to the job control form of work organization traditionally found in union plants.

Pay Concessions

In the face of intensified competition and large employment declines pay concessions were negotiated in a number of major collective bargaining agreements reached in 1982 and 1983.[1] These include the postponement and diversion of wage increases (to cover rising fringe benefit costs) in the rubber and trucking industries. Pay cuts or freezes were introduced in the meatpacking and steel industries, and at a number of airlines, including Braniff, Pan Am, American, United, and Eastern.

In a new master steel agreement covering seven major firms agreed to in February 1983, there was an immediate pay cut of $1.25 per hour, all of which is to be restored gradually over the duration of the forty-one-month agreement. In the new steel agreement the traditional COLA formula is retained (1 cent for each 0.3 point rise in the consumer price index), but the first five quarterly adjustments are eliminated, and there are limits on subsequent COLA payments. By the end of the contract, the full traditional COLA adjustments would be resumed.

In a revised national master freight agreement covering truck drivers and negotiated in March 1982, the traditional form of the COLA formula also was retained (1 cent for each 0.3 point increase in the consumer price index); however, nearly all of the COLA increases will be diverted to cover the rising costs of the fringe benefits provided in the truckers' contract. No other pay increases are provided over the thirty-one-month term of the new agreement.

The net effect of these pay cuts, freezes, and deferrals has been a marked slowing in the rise of compensation costs. Annual compensation adjustments in the United States over the life of the contract settlements covering 1,000 or more workers averaged 3.6 percent in 1982 and 2.8 percent in 1983 in contrast to the 7.9 percent rise in 1981 (U.S. Department of Labor 1983c, 1984).

These pay concessions sometimes involved a shift away from the use of COLA formula mechanisms and a shift to profit sharing or some other contingent compensation mechanisms that more directly tied pay to company performance. For example, a variable earnings plan was introduced at Braniff (prior to bankruptcy in 1981) and extended at Eastern Airlines in agreements covering the ground crew in 1982. When financial conditions continued to deteriorate at Eastern, wage cuts on the order of 20 percent were negotiated in 1983. In exchange Eastern employees received 25 percent of the airline's common stock and representation on its board of directors. A number of other financially distressed airlines, including Western Airlines, also introduced or proposed stock ownership plans as a way to raise sorely needed funds.

As in the auto industry, the general pattern followed in the pay concessions was that pay increases were first deferred or diverted to
cover the expense of rising fringe benefits. The trucking and steel
agreements are illustrations of this process. Yet the cumulative effect
of the pay concessions was to erode significantly the traditional use of
wage formulas.

Work Rule Concessions

The concessionary agreements negotiated in recent years often included major changes in work rules (Cappelli 1983b). For example,
new crew and hour limits were negotiated in a number of airlines,
and new work duties (requiring local pickups) were assigned to over-
the-road truck drivers. Work rule changes in the steel, airlines, rubber, and other industries in many cases involved a broadening of the
job classifications, a tightening of production standards, or some
other rule change that enabled management to adjust work assignments and work levels more flexibly (Katz 1984a; Kochan and Katz
1983; Kochan McKersie, and Cappelli 1984).

Decentralization of Bargaining

One of the effects of the concessionary agreements negotiated in
unionized industries has been to weaken traditional intraindustry
and interindustry pattern bargaining. For example, in the trucking
industry, the influence of the master freight agreement declined as
regional and company deviations from the national agreement
emerged. A number of financially distressed trucking firms chose to
ignore the national pay agreement. In the steel industry in the 1983
negotiations, the number of companies covered by the basic steel
agreement dropped from eight to seven (in the early 1960s the
number of firms covered was twelve).

Further erosion of pattern bargaining occurred in the steel industry in
1983 when the Wage Policy Committee of the United Steelworkers

(USW) established different bargaining goals for distressed industries such as basic steel and healthy industries such as nonferrous metal or containers where the USW also represented workers. This produced a weakening of the interindustry pattern bargaining that had traditionally characterized USW bargaining. There is now discussion of the possibility that in the 1985 negotiations, the basic steel agreement might be replaced by separate company agreements.

In many unionized industries a second form of decentralization has emerged through a downward shift in the level at which issues are resolved involving a movement from the national level to company- or plant-level resolution. For example, in the trucking industry, a number of financially distressed firms negotiated or imposed pay levels below the terms of the master freight agreement and also addressed other pay and work rule issues previously resolved exclusively in national bargaining. In the rubber and steel industries local bargaining also began to discuss and modify contract terms traditionally set and standardized at the national level (Cappelli 1982, 1983b). As pay setting shifted from national to local or company levels and pattern bargaining weakened, the influence that national unions traditionally played in pay determination lessened.

Worker Participation Programs and a Movement away from Job Control Unionism

In a number of industries there were also new cooperative programs at corporate and shop-floor levels. Many of these programs involve work rule changes and interact closely with other collective bargaining procedures and issues (Kochan, Katz, and Mower 1984; Kochan and Katz 1983). In some plants work team systems have been introduced that involve significant reductions in the number of job classifications and a movement away from reliance on traditionally detailed and formal procedures. In the plant where these worker participation programs took hold, the programs evolved away from an original narrow focus on housekeeping issues and increasingly began to address basic productivity and job security issues.

The evolution of the worker participation programs and the problems confronted in these plants are similar to the kinds of issues arising in the auto industry. The critical issue for the union was deciding how to mediate the relationship between worker participation programs and traditional collective bargaining procedures. In industries other than auto, a unique set of problems has been created by the rise of a nonunion alternative in these industries.

The opening of nonunion plants or subsidiaries has enabled management to pursue a double-edged labor relations strategy. On the one hand, the unionized facilities in these firms were introducing cooperative programs entailing increased worker and union involvement, team forms of work organization, and other movements away from job control unionism. At the same time, management was stimulating the growth of nonunion plants and introducing nontraditional labor relations practices in these nonunion plants. Even more important management was aggressively and largely successfully winning any union representation elections that occurred and maintaining the nonunion status of the plants. As a consequence of union representation election defeats and corporate investment and plant closing decisions, the number of nonunion plants is rising and the unions in many of these industries are seeing their membership decline steadily and significantly.[2]

Although the unions in these industries do not like the growth of nonunion operations, they often are helpless to stop it. In the process the unions and workers are torn between a desire to experiment with innovative labor relations practices as part of a recovery strategy and the fear that these practices might eventually combine with the growth of nonunion plants and lead to a rapid demise in union representation. Some unions are refusing to participate in concession or cooperative programs in unionized facilities on grounds that these actions are inconsistent with the simultaneous growth of nonunion operations within companies pursuing this sort of double-edged labor relations strategy (Kochan, McKersie, and Cappelli 1984).

The fact that some unions are reluctant to engage in cooperative programs where the threat of nonunion looms large points out an advantage the UAW had in its experimentation with work reorganization. The UAW has always had either complete or near-complete representation rights among auto blue-collar workers. Consequently, in contrast to unions and workers in many other industries, the UAW and autoworkers have less to fear regarding the possibility that the weakening of job control unionism will eventually bring an erosion of union representation rights. This may partly explain why the UAW has been willing to move relatively further along in worker participation programs and work organization experiments as compared to other unionized industries.

Although the growth in nonunion alternatives to collective bargaining has made unions suspicious of management's motives in workplace reforms, the economic success of nonunion operations has left union leaders with little choice but to experiment with workplace reforms or face even more rapid losses to the nonunion sector. An alternative strategy for these unions would be to organize the nonunion operations, but in most industries unions have been extremely unsuccessful in recent years in such organization campaigns (Farber 1984 and Freeman 1984).

In exchange for their acceptance of pay and work rule concessions, a number of unions have won new rights that expand their involvement in business decision making. Some unions have gained the right to receive information regarding business decisions or participate in decision making that was previously deemed to be a managerial prerogative (Cappelli, 1983a). Pan Am pilots were granted the right to elect a representative to sit on the corporate board of directors. In the rubber industry local union leaders and workers often have gained access to plant performance and business plans as part of their consideration of managerial demands for local work rule concessions (Cappelli 1983b).

In a number of cases unions have won some form of employment guarantee in exchange for pay and work rule concessions. American Airlines ground crews received job guarantees in exchange for their willingness to allow lower pay rates for new employees. United Airlines management agreed to a specific employment figure for pilots after pilots agreed to accept two-person crews in some aircraft. Plant-closing moratoriums were adopted in a number of meatpacking firms (Cappelli 1983b). As in the auto industry, the negotiation of these employment guarantees can be understood as part of the process by which management and union leaders convince workers that the pay and work rule concessions will bring a net expansion or at least no further reduction in employment.

Similarities between These Changes and Those in the Auto Industry

It would be inaccurate to argue that historically collective bargaining in most unionized industries in the United States used the exact terms of the three key features that structured bargaining historically in the auto industry. Few industries regularly include an annual improvement factor in their national agreements, and many unions operate in a more decentralized form than the auto industry, which led to more power in the hands of local unions and greater variation across companies and plants in contract terms. There are also many collective bargaining agreements that cover only one plant or region, a much more decentralized bargaining structure than that in the auto industry.

Yet in broad terms the labor relations system that operated in many unionized industries in the United States over the postwar period was very similar to that in the auto industry. Pattern bargaining across companies and industries and the heavy use of the COLA escalator functioned as a wage rule in an analogous manner to the wage formulas used in auto. In addition pattern bargaining and the important powers exercised by national unions (often through the grievance system) created a connective bargaining structure in many unionized industries (Bourdon 1979). Furthermore, nearly all unionized industries followed a job control orientation with heavy reliance on formal and arms-length rules and the linking of work duties and rights to detailed jobs (Piore 1982).[3] In industries where there was a major industrial collective bargaining agreement and a strong national industrial union such as steel and trucking, the similarity to the labor relations system found in autos is particularly strong.

Evidence that a well-connected labor relations system is operating in many unionized industries in a similar manner to the auto system is revealed by the way labor relations change has occurred in recent years in those industries. The concessions made in recent bargaining in these industries followed the same pattern as in auto by first introducing minor modifications to the key features of the labor relations in a manner that maintains each of those features and the structure of the traditional system. Formula wage increases were first deferred and then only supplemented by profit sharing or stock ownership schemes. Local work rule concessions were granted to special cases and deemed temporary adjustments. Worker participation programs were viewed as supplements to the collective bargaining process, and initially a sharp separation between these participation programs and so-called normal collective bargaining procedures was maintained.

And yet in a number of industries, just as in auto, the amendments made to the traditional labor relations system began to erode that system more seriously. For example, in the steel and other industries in a few plants, the worker participation programs began to introduce major changes to work organization and radically alter the role of local unions and workers by integrating them into decisions about technology, work area design, and production (Kochan, Katz, and Mower 1984, esp. chap. 4). In many industries local work rule concessions began to look less like exceptions to the national pattern and more like an avenue for major changes in collective bargaining (Kochan and Katz 1983).

Summary

Although the exact terms of the labor relations systems that operate in other unionized industries are not identical to the system in the auto industry, the conduct of labor-management relations is governed by a system in those industries. In those other industries, just as in the auto industry, the logic of the operation of a labor relations system implies that marginal changes are encouraged only to the extent that those changes do not jeopardize the basic terms of the system. Consequently in those industries, just as in the auto industry, future economic developments are likely to push labor and management toward paths that involve integrated and consistent changes in the various features of their labor relations systems.

The particular histories and specifics of labor-management relations in various industries will influence the future course of labor relations in those industries. Yet in broad terms the available choices are similar to the status quo, conflictual, or cooperative labor relations paths. The relationship between environmental economic conditions and these alternative paths also is likely to be similar to that in the auto industry. A critical difference in the role of environmental economic pressures, however, is that competitive cost pressure in the auto case primarily arises from heightened international competition, while other unionized industries face the additional pressures generated by domestic nonunion competition and, in some cases, deregulation.

Where economic pressures are extreme, the movement to nonunion alternatives or extensive outsourcing, and the conflict that is associated with the transition to those options, are more likely. Where buoyant economic conditions relieve the pressure for change, the attractiveness and inertia of the traditional labor relations system will favor its continuation.

As in the auto industry, in other industries facing moderately severe economic pressure labor and management will face the choice of pursuing either a status quo or cooperative path. For other industries the cooperative path has the same economic virtues it would provide to the auto industry: cost reduction and flexibility. In these other industries the cooperative option would entail the same basic elements as it would for the auto industry: compensation growth moderation and an increased reliance on contingent compensation; enhanced job security; more flexible work rules and team systems; and increased worker and union participation in decision making. As in the auto industry the difficult problem for labor and management if they head down the cooperative path, will be to develop an alternative labor relations system in which more flexible pay and work rule systems are integrated with new forms of worker and union participation. Meaningful work rule and worker participation processes will emerge only where no sharp distinction is drawn between improvements in the quality of working life and basic collective bargaining.

In the experimentation underway in other unionized industries, there is little evidence of the emergence of a full-fledged labor relations system that stands as an alternative to the traditional model. In fact most of these experiments are farther behind the innovations underway in parts of the auto industry; however, continuing pressure from nonunion competition, international competition, and in some cases deregulation is likely to lead other unionized industries in the United States to extend their search for less costly and more flexible production techniques. These industries will be hard pressed to find a way to compete with the new sophisticated nonunion model of personnel management. Unless the pace of innovation were to markedly increase in the auto industry, it appears that labor and management in other unionized industries will have to look elsewhere for a guide regarding how they can meet competitive challenges.

The success of the nonunion model of personnel management has stripped the auto industry of its role as the leading innovative sector in U.S. labor-management relations. In the years ahead, in their efforts to respond to environmental pressures, other unionized industries may well change their labor relations practices in ways that extend beyond the innovations underway in the auto industry. In the process the leadership role that the auto industry and the UAW have played in the unionized sector in the United States also would come to an end.

Describing the factors that will influence the course of labor relations in other industries would require a research effort much beyond this one. In particular, in industries where a critical aspect of labor relations is the growth of nonunion firms and hence the representation status of the workforce, one would have to assess the likely future course and influence of public policies affecting union status. One lesson is clear from the auto industry, that although the economic and public policy environment will shape the alternatives facing labor and management, and maybe even encourage movement in one direction or another, labor and management ultimately will make strategic choices that shape the course of labor relations.

Notes

Chapter 1

1. This figure includes employees engaged in the following activities: 1,117,000 in vehicle and parts manufacturing; 2,740,000 in automotive sales and servicing; 3,100,000 in truck driving and warehousing; 362,000 in passenger transportation; 456,000 in petroleum refining and production; and 278,000 in road construction (derived from U.S. Department of Transportation, 1982, table 17).

2. The role of strategic choice in labor relations is discussed in Piore and Sabel (1984); Kochan, McKersie, and Cappelli (1984); and Verma (1983). For a classic discussion of the ability of corporations to affect their environment, see Child (1972). For discussion of some of some of these issues in the British context, see Thurley and Wood (1983).

3. Dunlop (1958, p. ix) writes, "The central task of industrial relations is to explain why particular rules are established in particular industrial relations systems and how and why they change in response to changes affecting the system."

4. For example, see Piore (1982), Piore and Sabel (1984), Sabel (1982), Dore (1973), and Cole (1971, 1979).

5. Dunlop focuses on rules such as whether coal miners receive portal to portal pay and how construction workers are compensated during inclement weather (Dunlop, 1958, chaps. 5, 6).

6. Piore and Sabel (1984) also emphasize the role of historical and economic factors and downplay the importance of cultural factors in the development of institutional systems.

Chapter 2

1. A description of these three key dimensions also can provide a fruitful description of labor relations systems other than those in the U.S. auto industry. This point is addressed in more detail in chapter 7.

2. A chronology of contract negotiations in the auto industry is provided in Bureau of National Affairs (various years) and U.S. Department of Labor (1969, 1976).

3. The relationship between collective bargaining in the auto and other industries during World War II and the immediate postwar years is discussed in Lichtenstein (1982), Alexander (1959), Howe and Widick (1949), Reuther (1976), and Cormier and Eaton (1970).

4. The connections between these wage demands and Reuther's broader political agenda are discussed in Lichtenstein (1984).

5. The strength of interindustry pattern bargaining in the postwar period is discussed in Bourdon (1979) and in chapter 7.

6. The COLA and AIF formulas and the events surrounding their adoption are described in Ross (1949), Reder (1949), and Harbison (1950).

7. As wages and the consumer price index rose, the exact terms of the COLA formula were adjusted. In the 1979–1982 national auto contracts at GM and Ford, the COLA provided a one cent per hour wage increase for every 0.30 point increase in the national consumer price index until the third year of the agreement, when the formula was to be changed to one cent for each 0.26 increase.

8. The skilled trades problem is discussed in MacDonald (1963, pp.159–205).

9. A factor complicating the 1970 negotiations was the death of Walter Reuther. For a description of these negotiations, see Serrin (1973).

10. The AIF is described in the national contract in the following language: "The improvement factor provided herein recognizes that a continuing improvement in the standard of living of employees depends upon technological progress, better tools, methods, processes and equipment, and a cooperative attitude on the part of all parties in such progress. It further recognizes the principle that to produce more with the same amount of human effort is a sound economic and social objective." See section 101(b) of General Motors Corporation (1982).

11. Union versus nonunion wage differentials in the United States are traced in Mitchell (1980).

12. McPherson (1940) describes the earliest auto labor negotiations and agreements.

13. Strike statistics for the auto industry are reported in U.S. Department of Labor (1976, 1979).

14. The early history of the pressures for standardization is described in a letter from Irving Bluestone to the author, February 24, 1983.

15. The importance to labor unions of organizing the relevant product market is underscored in Ulman (1959).

16. This term is used by Piore (1982) and Piore and Sabel (1984) to describe how industrial unionism generally operates in the United States. I view the auto industry as a example of this pattern.

17. In contrast the labor relations systems in Japan and West Germany rely more on verbal and informal communication between labor and management. This point is discussed more fully in chapter 6.

18. An alternative to this system, discussed in more detail in chapter 6, is the Japanese auto industry where compensation is set heavily as a function of worker attributes, age, and skills, and only partially as a function of the nature of the job performed.

19. Descriptions of life on the auto assembly line are provided in Chinoy (1955) and Walker and Guest (1952).

20. Many of these practices followed procedures that had developed before the war in the garment, hosiery, and railroad industries (Harris 1982, p. 56; Millis and Montgomery 1945).

21. As with the earlier era, it is important to realize that events on the shop floor in the auto industry in this period were similar to what was occurring in many other unionized industries in the United States.

22. This and the following figure on local union demands come from unpublished internal files of General Motors Corporation.

Chapter 3

1. For example, in October 1982 the unemployment rates in the Detroit and Flint, Michigan, metropolitan areas were, respectively, 15.9 percent and 20.8 percent.

2. These are unpublished figures from the U.S. Department of Labor.

3. Imported motor vehicle sales figures are reported in MVMA (1982). Another indicator of the increased success of imports was that between 1978 and 1981, the constant dollar value of domestic sales by U.S. producers fell 36 percent while the value of import sales rose 24 percent (cited by Altshuler et al. 1984, p. 229).

4. The future prospects of the U.S. auto industry are reviewed in more detail in chapter 6. The many structural changes underway in the world automobile industry also are discussed more fully in Altshuler et al. (1984).

5. The figures in table 3.1 are consistent with those derived by the International Metalworkers Federation (1981). Similar figures for 1975 show that sizable wage differentials existed at that point as well and are not merely a reflection of the recent upward valuation of the U.S. dollar on international currency markets.

6. Chrysler's losses were $1.1 billion in 1979 and $1.7 billion in 1980 (Standard and Poors).

7. National contract settlements between each company and the UAW are summarized in Bureau of National Affairs (various years). One can also look at the detailed agreements such as the Ford Motor Company (1982a) and General Motors Corporation (1982).

8. This did not imply that Chrysler's hourly compensation costs were $2.50 below those at Ford and GM because with all of its layoffs Chrysler was forced to spread pension, health insurance, and other fringe benefit expenses, many of which were continuing for laid-off workers, over a smaller number of active workers.

9. By 1983 Ford and GM, respectively, had closed seven and five major plants.

10. In January 1982 Douglas Fraser (then president of the UAW) and Roger Smith (chairman of the board of GM) reached a tentative agreement that any later negotiated wage concessions would be linked to reductions in the price of cars at GM. This agreement later broke down, but it does provide further illustration of the union's and workers' need to see an explicit link between pay concessions and increased job security. The tentative agreement is described in Bureau of National Affairs (1982a).

11. For the differences in the profit-sharing formulas adopted at Ford and GM, see Bureau of National Affairs (1982c). In 1983 the profit-sharing plan paid out $440 per hourly worker at Ford and $640 per worker at GM.

12. The agreements include a limit on each company's potential total liability under the GIS program of $175 million at GM and $45 million at Ford.

13. An interesting feature of these programs is that they provide training and tuition assistance for programs that place laid-off autoworkers into jobs outside the auto industry. For details and examples of the Ford program, see UAW-Ford National Development and Training Center (1982).

14. The failure of these local negotiations is discussed in chapter 6.

15. The GM agreement speaks of "joint councils for enhancing job security and the competitive edge" (General Motors Corporation 1982, pp. 279–280) in place of Ford's "mutual growth forum" terminology (Ford Motor Company 1982b, pp. 29–34).

16. The Ford and GM 1982 contracts also included a number of other less significant changes. See Bureau of National Affairs (1982b, 1982c).

17. Shaiken (1982) and others criticized the removal of the paid personal holidays on grounds that the holidays generated net employment expansion and consequently their removal was inappropriate in light of the large number of layoffs in the industry as of 1982. However, the employment impacts of these holidays are not clear-cut and depend on whether one is speaking of the net addition of paid personal holidays to the contract or increases in the number of paid personal holidays made in lieu of increases in some other element of autoworkers' compensation and on the elasticity of demand for labor. Consider the case where paid personal holidays are a net addition to the autoworkers' fringe benefit package. This reduces the annual work hours of each autoworker but also raises hourly labor costs to the companies and, hence, the price of motor vehicles. The more elastic is the demand for motor vehicles, the more likely this leads to a net decline in the number of employed autoworkers due to a reduction in output that outweighs the employment effects produced by the reduction in autoworkers' annual work hours. However, if one is considering the case of choosing how to distribute any given increase in autoworkers' compensation, then increasing the number of paid personal holidays rather than increasing hourly pay rates does lead to greater employment. One would have to know the price elasticity of demand for labor to compute the magnitude of the net employment effects in either case.

18. Chrysler lost $69 million in 1982 and earned a profit of $700.9 million in 1983 (Standard and Poors).

19. The contract covering Canadian Chrysler workers (1982–1984) provides larger upfront wage increases, which ended the strict pattern following that historically had prevailed in the hourly wage rates paid Canadian and U.S. Chrysler workers.

20. The new contract also closed the gap that had emerged between pension benefits at Chrysler and those at Ford and GM.

21. My observations in this section are drawn from interviews conducted with union and management officials and workers in a number of plants between 1981 and 1984.

22. The sources of craft worker opposition to work reorganization are discussed more fully in chapter 4.

23. A clear statement of this view is presented in Farber (1978, in press).

24. The widespread adoption of significant local work rule changes and some of the problems created for union officials is described in Buss (1983).

Chapter 4

1. The early QWL programs and their motivation are discussed in Davis et al. (1975) and Walton (1979).

2. For Swedish management, the motivation for these programs was much the same as it was for the first generation of U.S. QWL programs: to deal with high absentee rates and alleged poor attitudes and lack of concern for quality among hourly workers. Swedish workplace experiments are reviewed in Agervold (1975). In the face of the economic success of Volvo and Saab in recent years, the primary motivation for the worker participation programs underway in those companies continues to be high worker turnover and absenteeism. See W. Peterson (1983). In contrast, in the United States, the second generation of QWL programs, which arose after 1979, was in response to the industry's poor economic condition, a very different source of motivation.

3. The history of the EI programs in Ford is traced in Ephlin (1983) and Savoie (1982).

4. This is another factor distinguishing the U.S. QWL programs from workplace reforms in Sweden where efforts to create alternatives to assembly-line-style production processes continued and to some degree expanded.

5. Later Bluestone supported the use of GM's operating team system, a system that clearly was more than a supplement to collective bargaining. His views about the team system are expressed in Bluestone (1983).

6. In 1971 GM's corporate industrial relations and personnel staff was split in two, creating a separate industrial relations department primarily handling issues relating to hourly workers and a personnel department handling issues related to salaried employees. The fact that the QWL group from which Warren was promoted was located in the personnel department at the time even though much of the focus of the programs was on hourly employees is revealing. This organizational structure reflected the industrial relations staff's dislike of QWL programs and the fact that the QWL programs were viewed as only a supplement to collective bargaining. Some of this history is noted in Cole (1979). Corporate staff responsibility for QWL programs in GM was moved to the corporate industrial relations department in 1982.

7. Examples of the views of workers opposed to cooperative programs are provided in Slaughter (1982, 1983) and Parker and Hansen (1983).

8. The responses to the whole survey are reported in Kochan, Katz, and Mower (1984).

9. Examples of team systems in nonunion plants are provided in Klein (1983) and Verma (1983).

10. Verma (1983) presents evidence regarding the spread of nonunion plants in one large conglomerate.

11. The plant performs operations very similar to those in Delco-Remy facilities located in Anderson, Indiana. Since Georgia is a right-to-work state, there exists no union shop clause in the Albany plant, and, in fact, a sizable number of the hourly work force do not belong to the UAW.

12. Rumor has it that in the GM-UAW national contract negotiations in 1976 and 1979, some of the pressure the union put on GM management to agree to the neutrality and accretion clauses involved a threat by UAW national leaders to reduce their support for QWL programs.

13. This fits the pattern described by Walton (1979) that greenfield sites are often used as a testing ground for organizational innovations.

14. There exists little evidence concerning the actual cost savings achieved by team systems.

15. The team system therefore could be viewed as a form of productivity bargain. For evidence regarding the use of buyouts in other productivity bargains, see Hartman (1969) and McKersie and Hunter (1973).

16. This is not always the case. At some team plants at certain times, the local union refused to participate on the planning committee.

17. This is an example of the diversity generally produced by QWL type programs. See Strauss (1980).

18. For discussion of whether management truly wants greater worker participation in decision making, see Witte (1980) and Berg, Freedman, and Freeman (1978).

19. In one team plant I visited, a majority of workers voted against the national agreement reached between GM and the UAW in the spring of 1982. Part of the reason for workers' rejection of the national contract may be that since this plant did not face the large layoffs occurring elsewhere, workers did not perceive the need for the pay concessions in the contract.

Chapter 5

1. This chapter draws heavily from Katz, Kochan, and Gobeille (1983) and Katz, Kochan, and Weber (in press).

2. The content analysis procedure used to score the QWL programs in division A is described in the appendix to this chapter.

3. The wide variation in industrial relations performance across these plants is consistent with the variation in industrial relations indicators Turner, Clack, and Roberts (1967) find in British auto plants, Pencavel (1974) finds in British coal mines, and Ichniowski (1983) finds in U.S. paper mills.

4. Commons (1921, p. 6) writes, "What about restrictions of output? Everybody knows that in good times working people 'lay down' on the job, whether organized or not. People do not work as hard in good times as they do in hard times."

5. In the regression analysis of data from division A, only grievance and absentee rates are included as industrial relations control variables. An alternative approach, and the one used in the analysis of division B data, would have included all of the industrial relations variables as control variables in the regression equation. Since a number of the industrial relations variables are missed for various plants and years in division A, this would have greatly

reduced the sample size in the regression. Grievance and absentee rates were included in the division A regressions because of the availability of these measures in nearly all the observations and because these variables measure key components of the industrial relations system.

6. For a discussion of potential statistical biases in models like this, see Butler and Ehrenberg (1981).

7. Correlations of data from plants within a given year consistently reveal an association between high product quality and low absentee rates.

8. An F test is performed on the set of dummy variables because F tests on individual plant dummy variables would vary as a function of whichever plant was used as the control group in this test.

9. Regression analysis has limitations as a test for QWL impacts. The regression specification focuses on the impacts the QWL programs in place in any given year in a plant exert on economic performance in that year. This specification may ignore some of the dynamic effects of QWL that accumulate over time. In addition selection problems associated with the diffusion of the QWL programs make it difficult to distinguish whether high-intensity QWL programs cause better industrial relations and economic performance or vice-versa. Furthermore it is extremely difficult under any circumstance to derive a good measure of the intensity and scope of the QWL programs underway in the plants. These complications motivate the use of various specifications in the regressions. At the same time the complications point out the value of supplementing the regression analysis with other analysis.

10. My reading of this evidence is consistent with Leibenstein (1976) who distinguishes between allocative and X-efficiency.

11. Evidence of modest positive impacts from QWL programs in the coal industry is also found in Goodman (1979).

Chapter 6

1. GM also has been negotiating with Daewoo Corporation of South Korea to produce a small car for export to the United States (Schiffman 1984).

2. Projections regarding future use of robots in the auto industry are provided in Hunt and Hunt (1982). For evidence regarding the implementation problems associated with the introduction of robotic technology, see Shaiken (1984).

3. The figure for the 1930s is reported in Abernathy (1978). The 1980 figure is from unpublished data from GM.

4. Auto demand forecasts are reviewed in U.S. Department of Transportation (1981); Altshuler et al. (1984); and Streeck and Hoff (1983a).

5. The UAW has been lobbying hard but unsuccessfully since 1980 for passage of local content legislation. For the UAW's arguments regarding the need for trade protection, see UAW (1980).

6. This table is a subset of the figures presented in table 9.5, Altshuler et al. (1984).

7. So far the UAW has not been able to organize production workers in Honda's Marysville, Ohio, motorcycle plant, which is next to the auto plant.

8. It is possible that at some point the UAW will succeed in organizing these plants. If that happens, it will be interesting to see if these plants follow a course similar to the Oklahoma City experience where the UAW bargained successfully for the removal of the team system in part because of the perception that the team system had been associated with the nonunion status of the plant.

9. This is an American variant of the neoliberal strategy described in Altshuler et al. (1984, chap. 9).

10. The implications of the growth in nonunion firms are discussed more fully in the next chapter.

11. This would amount to an acceleration of the recent trend toward increasing outsourcing.

12. For evidence that cooperative programs in the 1920s in the United States were more successful where the parties faced moderate economic pressure, see Jacoby (1983).

13. For a statement of the macroeconomic advantages of contingent forms of compensation, see Weitzman (1984).

14. For evidence regarding the rididity of wages in the United States relative to other member nations of the Organization for Economic and Cooperative Development, see Sachs (1979).

15. Evidence of a positive association between the cyclical volatility of production in an industry in Japan and the share of earnings paid in the form of bonuses is provided in Hashimoto (1979, table 4).

16. For evidence of a similar shortening of contract length in other industries, see Mitchell (1982).

17. There is a separate company pay agreement at Volkswagen since under federal law, due to its partial public ownership, Volkswagen is not allowed to join an employers' association. For more information on the West German auto industry, see Streeck and Hoff (1982, 1983b), from which my description draws heavily.

18. A similar pattern is revealed in figures comparing the total compensation (wages and fringes) received by autoworkers and production workers in all manufacturing industries. The ratio of autoworkers' and all manufacturing workers' total compensation in 1980 in the United States, West Germany, and Japan was, respectively, 1.65, 1.24, and 1.23. Figures derived from U.S. Department of Labor (1983c).

19. This is not to say that the Japanese labor relations system satisfies all workers' wants. For an account of the darker side of that system, see Kamata (1982). For the argument that the mutual cooperation derived through consultation in Japan often amounts to union "subordination to the authority of management," see Cole (1971, p. 260).

20. For a description of the limited personnel planning for blue-collar auto workers that occurs in the United States, see Katz and Karl (1983).

21. This figure was cited by Honda executives and union officials in interviews conducted in Tokyo in June 1982.

22. This section draws heavily from Streeck and Hoff (1982, pp. 345–346).

23. For a description of how employment stability is provided in West Germany, see Sengenberger and Kohler (1982). For Japan, see Cole (1971, 1979).

24. This has not led to the complete demise of Japanese autoworkers' fear of technological displacement. In 1983 the Nissan workers' union and Nissan management reached a formal agreement concerning the introduction of new technology. The agreement provides that no union members will be laid off or dismissed due to the introduction of new technology, and no downgradings or reductions in wages or working conditions will occur as a consequence of the introduction of new technology.

25. This can be viewed as an example of a dual labor market where workers in the secondary labor market absorb the burden of cyclical flux and thereby help to provide employment stability to workers in the primary sector. See Piore (1980).

26. For example, Nippon Kokan recently loaned more than two hundred workers from declining steel mills to Toyota Motor, Isuzu Motors, and Fugi Heavy Industries (Lohr 1984).

27. The course of negotiations in the pilot employment guarantee sites is reported in Warren (1983a, 1983b).

28. The strained tone of this relationship was described to me in interviews with GM executives and UAW officials.

29. For Ephlin's description of the relationship at Ford, see Ephlin (1983). Ford management's view is presented in Savoie (1982).

30. For example, see Caldwell (1983) and D. Peterson (1982).

31. For example, see Slaughter (1982).

32. A history of the internal affairs of the UAW is presented in Steiber (1962). For a more critical and, I think somewhat inaccurate view of the union, see Serrin (1973).

33. For details of the 1984 GM-UAW settlement, see UAW (1984).

34. Wages also differ across the Big Three because Chrysler's 1983–1985 contract with the UAW provides somewhat lower hourly wage rates.

35. The 1984–1987 contract also raises pension benefits and provides lump-sum payments to some workers who retire with less than 30 years service. By creating job openings by increasing retirement rates, these provisions may further limit GM's expenses under the new job security program.

36. The 1984 settlement included two other commitments that also might lead to the creation of new jobs for displaced autoworkers. GM management pledged to devote $100 million to new enterprises into which displaced auto-workers could be transferred and promised to consult with the union regarding outsourcing, although the specific consequences of these pledges remain unclear.

Chapter 7

1. My description of recent union concessions draws heavily from Katz (1984a) and has benefited greatly from discussions with Peter Cappelli, Thomas Kochan, and Robert McKersie.

2. A good illustration of how this occurred in one large conglomerate is provided in Verma (1983).

3. The labor relations systems operating in the construction and clothing industries do not fit this pattern. See Piore and Sabel (1984).

References

Abernathy, William J. 1978. *The Productivity Dilemma: Roadblock to Innovation in the Automobile Industry*. Baltimore: Johns Hopkins University Press.

Abernathy, William J., Kim B. Clark, and Alan M. Kantrow. 1981. "The New Industrial Competition." *Harvard Business Review* (September–October): 68–81.

Abernathy, William J., Kim B. Clark, and Alan M. Kantrow. 1983. *Industrial Renaissance*. New York: Basic Books.

Agervold, Mogens. 1975. "Swedish Experiments in Workplace Democracy." In Lou Davis et al. eds., *The Quality of Working Life*. New York: Free Press.

Alexander, Kenneth O. 1959. "Collective Bargaining in the Auto Industry." *Business Topics* 7, no. 2 (Spring): 59–70.

Altshuler, Alan et al. 1984. *The Future of the Automobile*. Cambridge: M.I.T. Press.

Berg, Ivar, Marcia Freedman, and Michael Freeman. 1978. *Managers and Work Reform: A Limited Engagement*. New York: Free Press.

Bluestone, Irving. 1980. "How Quality of Worklife Projects Work for the United Auto Workers." *Monthly Labor Review* (July).

Bluestone, Irving. 1983. "The Union Perspective." Epilogue to "The Business Team Approach," John J. Nora et al., eds. Unpublished manuscript.

Bourdon, Clinton. 1979. "Pattern Bargaining, Wage Determination, and Inflation: Some Preliminary Observations on the 1976–78 Wage Round." In *Unemployment and Inflation: Institutionalist and Structuralist Views*, Michael J. Piore, ed. White Plains, N.Y.: M. E. Sharpe.

Burck, Charles G. 1982. "Can Detroit Catch Up?" *Fortune*, February 8, pp. 34–45.

Bureau of National Affairs. Various years. "Collective Bargaining Negotiations and Contracts: Wage Patterns." Washington, D.C.

Bureau of National Affairs. 1982a. "General Motors Accepts Union Proposal to Pass Labor Costs Savings to Consumers." *Daily Labor Reports*, January 12, p. A-11.

Bureau of National Affairs. 1982b. "Joint UAW-Ford Summary of Terms of Tentative National Agreement." *Daily Labor Reports*, February 16, pp. El-E4.

Bureau of National Affairs. 1982c. "General Motors and Auto Workers Settle on Early Contract Following Ford Pattern." *Daily Labor Reports*, March 23, pp. AA-1, AA-2.

Bureau of National Affairs. 1982d. "Bieber Wins Endorsement to Succeed Fraser as Auto Workers President," *Daily Labor Reports*, November 12, p. A-12.

Bureau of National Affairs. 1983. "Auto Workers End Local Strike in Ohio That Idled Several Chrysler Corporation Plants." *Daily Labor Reports*, November 7, p. A-7.

Bureau of National Affairs. 1984. "Pilot Program to Guarantee Jobs Approved at Ford Plant in Michigan." *Daily Labor Reports*, March 15, p. A-5.

Business Week. 1964. "Brush Fires Plague Auto Industry." November 14, p. 54.

Business Week. 1982. "A Pact That May Make History." February 8, pp. 81–82.

Business Week. 1983a. "Detroit's Merry-Go-Round." September 12, pp. 72–77.

Business Week. 1983b. "Sales Are in for a Long, Lazy Climb." November 14, pp. 50–51.

Business Week. 1984a. "Ford's Better Idea South of the Border." January 23, pp. 43–44.

Business Week. 1984b. "Big Steel vs. The USW: The Lines Harden." January 30, pp. 84–85.

Business Week. 1984c. "The Vanishing All-American Small Car." March 12, pp. 88–91.

Business Week. 1984d. "Executive Pay: The Top Earners," May 7, 1984, pp. 88–95.

Buss, Dale D. 1983. "Unions Say Auto Firms Use Interplant Rivalry to Raise Work Quotas." *Wall Street Journal*, November 7, pp. 1, 31.

Buss, Dale D., and John Koten. 1983. "GM-Toyota Proposed Venture May Face Output Delays as It Awaits FTC Ruling." *Wall Street Journal*, September 23.

Butler, Richard J., and Ronald G. Ehrenberg. 1981. "Estimating the Narcotic Effect of Public Sector Impasse Procedures." *Industrial and Labor Relations Review* 35, no. 1 (October): 3–20.

Caldwell, Philip. 1983. "The Competitive Challenge to Business and Education." Speech to the Conference Board, September 26.

Cappelli, Peter. 1982. "Concession Bargaining and the National Economy." *Proceedings of the Thirty-Fifth Annual Meeting of the IRRA*. Madison: Industrial Relations Research Association.

Cappelli, Peter. 1983a. "Union Gains under Concession Bargaining." Unpublished manuscript. January.

Cappelli, Peter. 1983b. "Plant-Level Concession Bargaining and the Shutdown Threat." Unpublished manuscript, August.

Chamberlain, Neil. 1961. "Determinants of Collective Bargaining Structures." In *The Structure of Collective Bargaining*, A. Weber, ed. New York: Glencoe.

Child, John. 1972. "Organizational Structure, Environment and Performance: The Role of Strategic Choice." *Sociology* 6 (September): 1–22.

Chinoy, Ely. 1955. *Automobile Workers and the American Dream*. Garden City, N.Y.: Doubleday.

Cole, Robert E. 1971. *Japanese Blue Collar*. Berkeley and Los Angeles: University of California Press.

Cole, Robert E. 1979. *Work, Mobility and Participation*. Berkeley and Los Angeles: University of California Press.

Commons, John R. 1921. Introduction to *Trade Unions and Labor Problems*, John Commons, ed. 2d ed. Boston: Gin and Company.

Cormier, Frank, and William J. Eaton. 1970. *Reuther*. New Jersey: Prentice-Hall.

Cushman, Edward. 1961. "Management Objectives in Collective Bargaining." In *The Structure of Collective Bargaining*, A. Weber, ed. New York: Glencoe.

Davis, Lou et al., eds. 1975. *The Quality of Working Life.* New York: Free Press.

Dore, Ronald. 1973. *British Factory—Japanese Factory.* Berkeley and Los Angeles: University of California Press.

Dowling, William F. 1975. "System 4 Builds Performance and Profits." *Organizational Dynamics* 3, no. 3 (Winter): 23–37.

Dunlop, John T. 1958. *Industrial Relations Systems.* New York: Holt and Company.

Dunlop, John T. 1982. "Working toward Consensus." *Challenge* 25 (July–August): 26–34.

Edwards, Charles E. 1965. *The Dynamics of the American Auto Industry.* Columbia: University of South Carolina Press.

Ephlin, Donald F. 1983. "The UAW-Ford Agreement—Joint Problem Solving." *Sloan Management Review* (Winter): 61–65.

Farber, Henry S. In press. "The Analysis of Union Behavior." In *Handbook of Labor Economics*, O. Ashenfelter and R. Layard, eds. Amsterdam: North Holland.

Farber, Henry S. 1978. "Individual Preferences and Union Wage Determination: The Case of the United Mine Workers." *Journal of Political Economy* 86 (October): 923–942.

Farber, Henry S. 1984. "The Extent of Unionization in the United States: Historical Trends and Prospects for the Future." In *Challenges and Choices for American Labor*, T. A. Kochan, ed. Cambridge, Mass.: M.I.T. Press.

Ford Motor Company. 1979. "Agreements Between Ford Motor Company and the UAW."

Ford Motor Company. 1982a. "Agreements between Ford Motor Company and the UAW." February 13.

Ford Motor Company. 1982b. "Letters of Understanding between the Ford Motor Company and the UAW." February 13.

Foulkes, Fred K. 1980. *Personnel Policies in Large Nonunion Companies.* Englewood Cliffs, N.J.: Prentice-Hall.

Fox, Alan. 1974. *Beyond Contract: Work, Authority, and Trust Relations,* London: Macmillan.

Freedman, Audrey. 1982a. "A Fundamental Change in Wage Bargaining." *Challenge* 25 (July–August): 14–17.

Freedman, Audrey. 1982b. "Japanese Management of U.S. Work Forces." Research Bulletin 119. New York: Conference Board.

Freeman, Richard B. 1984. "Why Are Unions Fairing So Poorly in NLRB Representation Elections." In *Challenges and Choices for American Labor*, T. A. Kochan, ed. Cambridge, Mass.: M.I.T. Press.

Galenson, Walter. 1976. "The Japanese Labor Market." In *Asia's New Giant*, H. Patrick and H. Rosovsky, eds. Washington, D.C.: Brookings Institution.

Garbarino, Joseph W. 1959. "The Economic Significance of Automatic Wage Adjustments." In *New Dimensions in Collective Bargaining*, Harold W. Davey, ed. New York: Harper and Brothers.

General Motors Corporation. 1976. "Local Agreements, Understandings, Statements of Policy and General Information." Framingham Plant.

General Motors Corporation. 1982. "Agreement between General Motors Corporation and the UAW."

Goodman, Paul S. 1979. *Assessing Organizational Change: The Rushton Quality of Work Experiment.* New York: Wiley-Interscience.

Guest, Robert H. 1979. "Quality of Work Life—Learning from Tarrytown." *Harvard Business Review* 57 (July–August): 76–87.

Harbison, Frederick H. 1950. "The General Motors-United Auto Workers Agreement of 1950." *Journal of Political Economy* 58, (October): 397–411.

Harbison, Frederick H., and Robert Dubin. 1947. *Patterns of Union-Management Relations.* Chicago: Science Research Associates.

Harris, Howell John. 1982. *The Right to Manage.* Madison: University of Wisconsin Press.

Hartman, Paul. 1969. *Collective Bargaining and Productivity: The Longshoring Mechanization Agreement.* Berkeley: University of California Press.

Harvard Business School. 1976. "General Motors Corporation—Detroit Plant." Case 9-676-072. Cambridge: Harvard Case Clearing House.

Hashimoto, Masanori. 1979. "Bonus Payments, On-the Job Training, and Lifetime Employment in Japan." *Journal of Political Economy.* 87, no. 5 (October): 1086–1104.

Herding, Richard. 1972. *Job Control and Union Structure: A Study on Plant-Level Industrial Conflict in the United States*. Rotterdam: Rotterdam University Press.

Holusha, John. 1983a. "U.A.W. Wins Recognition at Coast G.M.-Toyota Plant." *New York Times*, September 23.

Holusha, John. 1983b. "Chevy Turns to the Japanese." *New York Times*, October 6.

Howe, Irving, and B. J. Widick. 1949. *The UAW and Walter Reuther*. New York: Random House.

Hoxie, Robert F. 1920. *Trade Unionism in the United States*. New York: D. Appleton and Company.

Hunt, H. Allan, and Timothy L. Hunt. 1982. *Robotics: Human Resource Implications for Michigan*. Kalamazoo, Mich.: W. E. Upjohn Institute for Employment Research.

Ichniowski, Bernard E. 1983. "How Do Labor Relations Matter?" Ph.D. dissertation, M.I.T.

Inagami, Takeshi. 1983. *Labor-Management Communications at the Workshop Level*. Tokyo: Japanese Institute of Labour.

International Metalworkers Federation. 1978. "International Comparison of Wages and Working Conditions." Report prepared for the International Metalworkers Federation World Auto Conference, Detroit, Michigan.

Jacoby, Sanford M. 1983. "Union-Management Cooperation in the United States: Lessons from the 1920s." *Industrial and Labor Relations Review* 37, no. 1 (October): 18–33.

Kamata, Satoshi. 1982. *Japan in the Passing Lane*. New York: Random House.

Kassalow, Everett. 1981. "Collective Bargaining: In the Grip of Structural Change?" *Proceedings of the Thirty-third Annual Meeting of the IRRA*. Madison: Industrial Relations Research Association.

Katz, Harry C. 1984a. "Collective Bargaining in 1982: A Turning Point in Industrial Relations?" *Compensation Review* 16, no. 1 (First Quarter): 38–49.

Katz, Harry C. 1984b. "The U.S. Automobile Collective Bargaining System in Transition." *British Journal of Industrial Relations* 22, no. 2 (July).

Katz, Harry C., and Charles F. Sabel. 1979. "Wage Rules: A Theory of Wage Determination." Paper presented to the Annual Econometric Society Meetings, Atlanta, Georgia December.

Katz, Harry C., Thomas A. Kochan, and Kenneth R. Gobeille. 1983. "Industrial Relations Performance, Economic Performance and QWL Programs: An Interplant Analysis." *Industrial and Labor Relations Review* 37, no. 1 (October): 3–17.

Katz, Harry C., Thomas A. Kochan, and Mark Weber. In press. "Assessing the Effects of Industrial Relations and Quality of Working Life Efforts on Organizational Effectiveness." *Academy of Management Journal.*

Katz, Harry C., and Ron Karl. 1983. "Personnel Planning in the U.S. Auto Industry." In *Workforce Restructuring, Manpower Management and Industrial Relations in the World Automobile Industry,* W. Streeck and A. Hoff, eds. Berlin: International Institute for Management, Science Center.

Kerr, Clark, et al. 1960. *Industrialism and Industrial Man.* Cambridge: Harvard University Press.

Klein, Janice. 1983. "First Line Supervisor Resistance to Worker Participation Programs." Ph.D. dissertation, M.I.T.

Kochan, Thomas A., and Peter Cappelli. 1984. "The Transformation of the Industrial Relations and Personnel Function." In *Internal Labor Markets,* Paul Osterman, ed., Cambridge: M.I.T. Press.

Kochan, Thomas A., Harry C. Katz, and Nancy Mower. 1984. *Worker Participation and American Unions: Threat or Opportunity?* Kalamazoo, Mich.: W. E. Upjohn Institute for Employment Research.

Kochan, Thomas, and Harry C. Katz, 1983. "Collective Bargaining, Work Organization and Worker Participation: The Return to Plant Level Bargaining." *Labor Law Journal* 34 (August): 524–530.

Kochan, Thomas, and Robert B. McKersie. 1983. "Collective Bargaining— Pressures for Change." *Sloan Management Review* 24, no. 4 (Summer): 59–65.

Kochan, Thomas, Robert B. McKersie, and Peter Cappelli. 1984. "Strategic Choice and Industrial Relations Theory." *Industrial Relations* (Winter): 16–39.

Koshiro, Kazutoshi. 1982. "Industrial Relations in the Japanese Automobile Industry." In *Industrial Relations in the World Automobile Industry: The Experiences of the 1970s,* W. Streeck and A. Hoff, eds. Berlin: International Institute for Management, Science Center.

Koshiro, Kazutoshi. 1983. "Personnel Planning, Technological Change, and Outsourcing in the Japanese Automobile Industry." In *Workforce Restructuring Manpower Management and Industrial Relations in the World Automobile Industry,*

W. Streeck and A. Hoff, eds. Berlin: International Institute for Management, Science Center.

Koten, John. 1981. "Ford Decides Bigness Isn't a Better Idea." *Wall Street Journal,* September 16, p. 29.

Kuhn, James W. 1961. *Bargaining and Grievance Settlement.* New York: Columbia University Press.

Leibenstein, Harvey. 1976. *Beyond Economic Man: A New Foundation for Microeconomics,* Cambridge: Harvard University Press.

Levinson, Harold M. 1960. "Pattern Bargaining: A Case Study of the Automobile Workers." *Quarterly Journal of Economics* 74, no. 2 (May): 296–317.

Lichtenstein, Nelson. 1980. "Auto Worker Militancy and the Structure of Factory Life, 1937–1955." *Journal of American History* 67, no. 2 (September): 335–353.

Lichtenstein, Nelson. 1982. *Labor's War at Home.* London and New York: Cambridge University Press.

Lichtenstein, Nelson. 1984. "Reutherism on the Shop Floor: UAW Bargaining Strategy and Shop Floor Control in the U.S. 1946–1970." Presented at the International Conference on the Automobile Industry: Past, Present and Future, Coventry, England, June 28–July 1.

Lohr, Steve. 1984. "A Critical Shift for Japan's Steel Industry." *New York Times,* March 20.

MacDonald, Robert M. 1963. *Collective Bargaining in the Automobile Industry.* New Haven: Yale University Press.

McKersie, Robert B., and Laurence C. Hunter. 1973. *Pay, Productivity and Collective Bargaining.* London: Macmillan Press.

McPherson, William H. 1940. *Labor Relations in the Automobile Industry.* Washington, D.C.: Brookings Institution.

Millis, Harry A., and Royal E. Montgomery. 1945. *Organized Labor.* New York: McGraw-Hill.

Mitchell, Daniel J. B. 1980. *Unions, Wages and Inflation.* Washington, D.C.: Brookings Institution.

Mitchell, Daniel J. B. 1982. "Recent Union Contract Concessions." *Brookings Papers on Economic Activity,* no. 1. Washington, D.C.: Brookings Institution.

Montgomery, David. 1980. *Workers Control in America*. London: Cambridge University Press.

MVMA. 1981. *MVMA Motor Vehicle Facts and Figures*. Detroit: Motor Vehicle Manufacturers Association.

Parker, Mike, and Dwight Hansen. 1983. "The Circle Game." *Progressive* (January): 32–35.

Pencavel, John H. 1974. "Analysis of an Index of Industrial Morale." *British Journal of Industrial Relations* 12 (March): 48–55.

Peterson, Donald. 1982. "The Second Bottom Line: A Discussion of the Historic Ford-UAW Contract." Speech to the Sloan School of Management, MIT, Distinguished Speakers Series, April 1.

Peterson, William. 1983. "Personnel Planning in the Swedish Automobile Industry." In Streeck and Hoff (1983b).

Piore, Michael J. 1980. "Dualism as a Response to Flux and Uncertainty." In *Dualism and Discontinuity in Industrial Societies*, S. Berger and M. Piore, eds. Cambridge University Press.

Piore, Michael J. 1982. "American Labor and the Industrial Crisis." *Challenge* 25, no. 2 (March–April): 5–11.

Piore, Michael J., and Charles F. Sabel. 1984. *The Second Industrial Divide*. New York: Basic Books.

Reder, Melvin W. 1949. "The Significance of the 1948 General Motors Agreement." *Review of Economics and Statistics* 31 (February 1949): 7–14.

Reuther, Victor G. 1976. *The Brothers Reuther and the Story of the UAW: A Memoir*. Boston: Houghton Mifflin.

Rothchild, Emma. 1973. *Paradise Lost: The Decline of the Auto-Industrial Age*. New York: Random House.

Ross, Arthur M. 1948. *Trade Union Wage Policy*. Berkeley and Los Angeles: University of California Press.

Ross, Arthur M. 1949. "The General Motors Wage Agreement of 1948." *Review of Economics and Statistics* 31 (February): 1–7.

Rotbart, Dean. 1983. "American Air's New Contract with Union Seen Aiding Other Carriers in Labor Talks." *Wall Street Journal*, March 7.

Sabel, Charles F. 1982. *Work and Politics.* Cambridge: Cambridge University Press.

Sachs, Jeffery D. 1979. "Wages, Profits, and Macroeconomic Adjustment: A Comparative Study." *Brookings Papers on Economic Activity,* no. 2 Washington, D.C.: Brookings Institution.

Salpukas, Agis. 1984. "A Restructured Steel Industry." *New York Times,* February 2.

Savoie, Ernest J. 1982. "The New Ford-UAW Agreement: Its Worklife Aspects." *Worklife Review* 1, 1 (July): 2–12.

Schiffman, James R. 1984. "GM, Daewoo See Signing Car-Making Pact." *Wall Street Journal,* March 1.

Selekman, Benjamin M. et al. 1964. *Problems in Labor Relations.* 3d ed. New York: McGraw-Hill.

Sengenberger, W., and Ch. Kohler. 1982. "Policies of Work Force Reduction and Labour Market Structures in the American and German Automobile Industry." Paper presented to the Annual Conference of the International Working Party on Labor Market Segmentation, Modena, Italy, September 7–11.

Serrin, William. 1973. *The Company and the Union.* New York: Knopf.

Shaiken, Harley. 1982. "At Stake in Detroit." *New York Times,* January 21.

Shaiken, Harley. 1984. *Automation and Workplace: Case Studies on the Introduction of Programmable Automation in Manufacturing.* Washington, D.C.: Office of Technology Assessment.

Slaughter, Jane. 1982. "Opposition Grows as Auto Union Pushes Concessions at GM and Ford." *Labor Notes,* January 21.

Slaughter, Jane. 1983. "Auto Workers Find Concessions Didn't Buy Job Security." *Labor Notes,* March 29.

Slichter, Sumner, James J. Healey, and Robert Livernash. 1960. *The Impact of Collective Bargaining on Management.* Washington, D.C.: Brookings Institution.

Standard and Poors. Various years. *Stock Reports.*

Steiber, Jack. 1962. *Governing the UAW.* New York: Wiley.

Strauss, George. 1962. "The Shifting Power Balance in the Plant." *Industrial Relations* 2 (October): 65–96.

Strauss, George. 1980. "Quality of Worklife and Participation as Bargaining Issues." In *The Shrinking Perimeter*, Hervey A. Juris and Myron Roomkin, eds. Lexington, Mass.: Lexington Books.

Streeck, Wolfgang. 1981. "Qualitative Demands and the Neo-Corporatist Manageability of Industrial Relations." *British Journal of Industrial Relations* 19, no. 2 (July): 149–169.

Streeck, Wolfgang. 1984. *Industrial Relations in West Germany: A Case Study of the Car Industry*. New York: St. Martin's Press.

Streeck, Wolfgang, and Andreas Hoff. 1982. "Industrial Relations in the German Automobile Industry: Developments in the 1970s." In W. Streeck and A. Hoff, eds., *Industrial Relations in the World Automobile Industry—The Experiences of the 1970s*. Berlin: International Institute for Management, Science Center.

Streeck, Wolfgang, and Andreas Hoff. 1983a. *Industrial Adjustment and the Structure of Employment in the Automobile Industry*. Report to the European Economic Commission. Berlin: International Institute for Management, Science Center.

Streeck, Wolfgang, and Andreas Hoff. 1983b. *Workforce Restructuring, Manpower Managment and Industrial Relations in the World Automobile Industry*. Report to the European Economic Commission. Berlin: International Institute for Management, Science Center.

Thurley, Keith, and Stephen Wood. 1983. *Industrial Relations and Management Strategy*. London: Cambridge University Press.

Turner, H. A., Garfield Clack, and Geoffrey Roberts. 1967. *Labour Relations in the Motor Industry*. London: Allen and Urwin.

Ulman, Lloyd. 1959. *The Rise of the National Trade Union*. Cambridge: Harvard University Press.

Ulman, Lloyd, 1974. "Connective Bargaining and Competitive Bargaining." *Scottish Journal of Political Economy* 21, no. 2 (June): 97–109.

UAW. 1980. "Petition for Relief under Section 201 of the Trade Act of 1974 from Import Competition from Imported Passenger Cars, Light Trucks, Vans, and Utility Vehicles." Before the United States International Trade Commission, June 12.

UAW. 1984. "UAW-GM Report," September 1984, UAW Publications Department.

UAW-Ford National Development and Training Center. 1982. "Establishing a Local UAW-Ford Employee Development and Training Program—A Guide for Local Unions and Management." September.

U.S. Department of Health, Education and Welfare. Special Task Force. 1973. *Work in America*. Cambridge, Mass.: M.I.T. Press.

U.S. Department of Labor. 1969. "Wage Chronology—General Motors Corporation 1939–68." Bulletin 1532. Washington, D.C.: Bureau of Labor Statistics.

U.S. Department of Labor. 1976. "Collective Bargaining in the Motor Vehicle and Equipment Industry." Report 479. Washington, D.C.: Bureau of Labor Statistics.

U.S. Department of Labor 1979a. "Ford Motor Wage Chronology," Bulletin 1994, Washington, D.C.: Bureau of Labor Statistics.

U.S. Department of Labor. 1979b. "Collective Bargaining in the Motor Vehicle and Equipment Industry." Report 574. Washington, D.C.: Bureau of Labor Statistics.

U.S. Department of Labor. 1983a. "Hourly Compensation Costs for Production Workers in Motor Vehicles and Equipment Manufacturing, 17 Countries, 1975–1982." Unpublished series. Washington, D.C.: Bureau of Labor Statistics, Office of Productivity and Technology.

U.S. Department of Labor. 1983b. "Hourly Compensation Costs for Production Workers in Manufacturing 34 Countries, 1975–1982." Unpublished series. Washington, D.C.: Bureau of Labor Statistics, Office of Productivity and Technology.

U.S. Department of Labor. 1983c. "Major Collective Bargaining Settlements in Private Industry, 1982." Bulletin 83-41. Washington, D.C.: Bureau of Labor Statistics.

U.S. Department of Labor. 1983d. *Handbook of Labor Statistics*. Washington, D.C.: Bureau of Labor Statistics.

U.S. Department of Labor. 1984. "Major Collective Bargaining Settlements in Private Industry 1983." Bulletin 84-30. Washington, D.C.: Bureau of Labor Statistics.

U.S. Department of Labor. Various years. *Employment and Earnings*. Washington, D.C.: Bureau of Labor Statistics.

U.S. Department of Transportation. 1981. *The U.S. Automobile Industry, 1980.* Report to the President from the Secretary of Transportation. Washington, D.C., January.

U.S. Department of Transportation. 1982. *National Transportation Statistics,* Washington, D.C.: U.S. Government Printing Office.

Verma, Anil. 1983. "Union and Non-union Industrial Relations Systems at the Plant Level." Ph.D. Dissertation, M.I.T.

Walker, Charles R., and Robert Guest. 1952. *The Man on the Assembly Line.* Cambridge: Harvard University Press.

Wall Street Journal. 1982. "GM Agrees to Forgo Richer Bonus Pay after UAW Objects." April 23.

Walton, Richard E. 1979. "Work Innovations in the United States." *Harvard Business Review* 57 (July–August): 88–98.

Walton, Richard E., and Robert B. McKersie. 1965. *A Behavioral Theory of Labor Negotiations.* New York: McGraw-Hill.

Walton, Richard E., and Leonard Schlesinger. 1979. "Do Supervisors Thrive in Participative Work Systems?" *Organizational Dynamics* 7, 3 (Winter): 25–38.

Ward's. 1980. *Ward's Automotive Reports.* August 11, Detroit: Ward's Communication.

Ward's. (various years). *Ward's Automotive Yearbook.* Detroit: Ward's Communication.

Warren, James. 1983a. "Lifetime Job Pact at Ford." *Chicago Sun-Times,* March 13.

Warren, James. 1983b. "Ford Pact Rejected Here." *Chicago Sun-Times,* March 19.

Weber, Arnold. 1961. Introduction to *The Structure of Collective Bargaining,* A. Weber, ed. New York: Glencoe.

Weitzman, Martin L. 1984. *The Share Economy.* Cambridge: Harvard University Press.

Witte, John F. 1980. *Democracy, Authority and Alienation in Work: Workers' Participation in an American Corporation.* Chicago: Chicago University Press.

Index